Vandaleur's Folly

'Vandaleur was an Irish land-owner in the 1830s who turned his estate into an agricultural co-operative. His folly was to lose it again as a gambling debt. It is an ideal subject for Margaretta D'Arcy and John Arden with its rich political implications and its intrinsically melodramatic nature, and they present the action in a typically complex and ambivalent way.'

Jeremy Treglown, *The Times*

'The play is described as "an Anglo-Irish melodrama" and comes complete with footlights, false proscenium and multi-coloured backdrops. But inside the simple form we have a complex play about "the furious contradiction of Ireland". . . . Arden and D'Arcy also have the gift for writing a heightened prose that shades almost imperceptibly into song and ballad.'

Michael Billington, *Guardian*

Vandaleur's Folly was first staged by the 7:84 Theatre Company in autumn 1978 in a production which toured England and Ireland.

plays by John Arden and Margaretta D'Arcy

THE BUSINESS OF GOOD GOVERNMENT
THE ROYAL PARDON
THE HERO RISES UP
THE ISLAND OF THE MIGHTY

plays by John Arden

SERJEANT MUSGRAVE'S DANCE
THE WORKHOUSE DONKEY
ARMSTRONG'S LAST GOODNIGHT
PEARL

also available

PLAYS: ONE
(Serjeant Musgrave's Dance, The Workhouse Donkey,
Armstrong's Last Goodnight)

VANDALEUR'S FOLLY

An Anglo-Irish Melodrama
The Hazard of Experiment in an Irish
Co-operative, Ralahine, 1831

BY
MARGARETTA D'ARCY
AND
JOHN ARDEN

EYRE METHUEN

LONDON

First published in Great Britain in 1981 by
Eyre Methuen Ltd
11 New Fetter Lane
London EC4P 4EE

CAUTION

Set in IBM 10pt Journal by 𝍐 Tek-Art, Croydon, Surrey

Printed and bound in Great Britain by Fakenham Press Limited, Fakenham, Norfolk

PREFACE

In this play we tell the true story of how an agricultural co-operative commune was set up in the west of Ireland in 1831, how it succeeded beyond all possible expectation, and how just two years after its foundation it collapsed in a sudden and personal disaster just like the denouement of a melodrama of the same period. We also show how the ultimate failure of Ralahine (due to the original proprietor's retention of the legal ownership of the estate) reflected a particular flaw in Robert Owen's Utopian theory of Socialism — the theory which had inspired John Scott Vandaleur when he first heard it outlined by Owen at his famous Rotunda meeting in Dublin (1823). Owen's comparative naivety about the moral idealism of proprietors has already been challenged by William Thompson in 1822:

> 'No high-sounding moral maxims influence the rich as a body. A few individuals may rise above the impulse of their class . . . but the rich as a class . . . must acquire the inclinations and the characters, good or bad, which spring out of the state of things surrounding them from their birth.'

If this had been thoroughly understood when the Ralahine Experiment was embarked upon, Vaudaleur's 'inclination' towards the gaming-tables — themselves a notorious symptom of the social irresponsibility of the Anglo-Irish landlord class of the time — need never have been allowed to destroy both him and his enlightened project.

Thompson plays only a sideways role in our story: he was, historically, a sympathetic observer of the Ralahine Commune, and his own endeavours to create a similar co-operative in County Cork were so hampered by his careful insistence on

getting the theory completely correct from the very beginning
(extremely difficult, given the restrictive nature of the property
laws) that he died before anything concrete could be put in
hand, and all his resources disappeared in legal wranglings over
the validity of his will. But his importance as a revolutionary
thinker should not be under-estimated. James Connolly said of
him in his classic *Labour in Irish History* (1910):

> 'An economist more thoroughly socialist in the modern sense
> than any of his contemporaries . . . superior to any of the
> Utopian Socialists of the Continent, and long ante-dating
> Karl Marx in his insistence upon the subjection of Labour as
> the cause of all social misery, modern crime and political
> dependence, as well as in his searching analysis of the
> true definition of capital.'

Thompson's reputation has been somewhat obscured by later
writers, partly — one cannot help feeling — because Robert Owen,
as the central guru of the movement, with his main headquarters
in Britain, and a busy press promulgating his own theories, was
not inclined to afford him the publicity for ideas which
disturbed doctrinal consensus. As an Irishman Thompson
suffered already from a geographical and cultural
'off-shoredness': as an uncompromising revolutionist he
seemed out of place in a reformist intellectual climate. Marx
knew his work and was to build upon it: but Marx's international
impact was so enormous that his 'sources', like Shakespeare's,
tended to disappear from the public view. Yet just as one can
learn a great deal about, say, *Antony and Cleopatra* or *Timon
of Athens* by reading Plutarch, so British Marxists today who
find themselves bewildered in their attempts to understand
Irish revolutionary movements and organisations would do well
to study Thompson. It is appalling, though typical, that the
principal work upon him (by R.K.P. Pankhurst, 1954) should
refer to him in the sub-title as a 'British' Socialist. Thus the
colonial mentality enfolds all the achievements of subject
peoples into the suffocating embrace of the 'mother-country',
even when purporting to administer the elixir of liberation.

Anna Wheeler, Thompson's companion and collaborator, has similarly slipped almost out of sight. Yet she was a pioneer feminist of great influence in her own time: and the exuberantly-entitled book which she wrote with Thompson — the *Appeal of One Half of the Human Race, Women, against the Pretensions of the other Half, Men* — advocating, amongst other things, birth control, and family planning, was regarded as marking a highly significant step forward from Mary Wollstonecraft's previous statement of the case for women's liberation. We have been unable to do anything like proper justice to this remarkable woman in our play: she still awaits her biographer.

We do not pretend to have written a 'documentary play', although the main events in the story are all taken from E.T. Craig's eye-witness account of Ralahine, *An Irish Commune*. We have telescoped his narrative here and there, but in general have kept as close to the recorded facts as we could. We did however find it necessary to resort to unashamed invention in one principal area of the plot — the motivation for the catastrophe in the gambling-club. No-one knows exactly what caused Vandaleur to risk everything so insanely on the turn of the cards: to say simply his 'class-background' is inadequate for dramaturgy: not every landlord after all was so totally lacking in personal steadfastness. We decided (a) that he could have been mentally deranged, in which case the class-nature of the events would have been muffled by the pathology, and his original notion of the co-operative would have seemed far more whimsical than in fact it was; or (b) that he was a complete hypocrite, pursuing his own pleasures regardless of his responsibilities, which did not appear consistent with all else that is known of him: or (c) that someone 'fitted him up'. Now Craig does talk about certain neighbouring gentry who disapproved of the commune, and particularly resented the checking of the fox-hunt.

In order to discover just what kind of disapproval and resentment would have been involved, one must look beyond the obvious *class*-differences between gentry and tenants, and examine the whole situation of the Anglo-Irish colonial planter-families at the period, their Protestant religion, their Orange/Loyalist politics, and their attitude towards the Catholic peasantry as it emerged as a political force under O'Connell in the generations subsequent to the Act of Union (1800). In other words, imperialism impinges upon the straightforward picture of overweening property confronted by underprivileged labour: and Major Baker-Fortescue rears himself up as an essential character in the tale. At that time, as indeed today, Orange Loyalism was a sort of lunatic confusion of fear and fury, endeavouring to hold on to its ill-gotten Irish gains by interfering in British Politics, coercing, blackmailing, pleading for pity with a whingeing poor-mouth, and in the end imposing its own constant veto — always with the threat of violence — upon any enlightened attempt to improve the situation. Perhaps Baker-Fortescue seems exaggerated to modern audiences outside Ireland: his outbursts however can be paralleled by many well-documented historical accounts, and something very like them may be heard on TV every time a North of Ireland Loyalist politician is encouraged to display himself.

Baker-Fortescue is an invented person: so is Roxana, so is Wilberforce: and the whole of the slave-trade sub-plot was introduced out of our imagination in order to make clear the relationship between imperialist dealings in Ireland and in other parts of the world, and the racialist complications that have been the result of them. The characters of Roisin and Micheal are fictional too: we have merely given names and faces to the anonymous peasants Craig talks about, with their secret societies, their killings and intimidations; and their enthusiastic acceptance of the idea of a co-operative, once its genuine potential had been thoroughly tested. The hunt that the Ralahine communards balked was in reality in pursuit of foxes, not women; but there is a persistent folk-tradition in many parts of Ireland that the gentry did hunt their servant-maids in the way we have shown: and by the time we reached the beginning of Act Two we discovered Baker-Fortescue had attained such a height of barbarity that the logic of melodrama seemed to demand the modification of the story.

The historical persons in the play are the following: Thompson, Anna, Hastings, Mr and Mrs Vandaleur, the Lord Mayor and Archbishop, Robert Owen, Craig. Craig's summing-up speech in the Epilogue (beginning 'Ralahine had been an Irish point of interrogation . . .') is a deliberately anachronistic quote from James Connolly. The Duke of Cumberland's unsuccessful Orange/Tory coup against Queen Victoria's accession to the throne is a piece of 'mythological history', perhaps true, perhaps not: but dismissed by too many historians a little too easily ('such things don't really happen in Britain: so it has to be leftist paranoia . . .'). If there was indeed such an attempt, it might well have left no traces, the British Establishment being what it is.

When we first embarked on the play we thought of it as a useful contribution to a better understanding of Anglo-Irish conflict: how reformist advances have continually been set back by aggressive reaction, driving the Irish people again and again to 'terrorist' methods: and how this process has so constantly been connived at and assisted by the blindness to their own inbred imperialism of even the most progressive British political and social groups. It was to be presented by the English 7:84 Company, an organisation devoted — as its name suggests — to attacking the capitalist structure of society by means of theatre brought primarily to the working classes. Such a company possesses an internal constitution of a co-operative kind, and in theory is composed of actors and backstage staff who all subscribe to the ideas that are to be put forward in the plays. We did not realise until we started active work on the text with the company just how closely the difficulties of the enterprise would parallel those of Edward Craig at Ralahine.

Where Vandaleur had put his own money and property into the commune that Craig organised, and thus retained a crucial and fatal control over its destiny, so the contemporary Socialist theatre-group receives its funds from the Arts Council, and finds all its efforts subject to the limitations of this patronage. Of recent years the Arts Council has demanded more and more observable financial success from the companies: dates in specifically working-class venues have imperceptibly been dropped in favour of apolitical community centres, arts institutes, and the like. The schedule of the tours has been intensified to such a degree that the jaded performers are bundled out on the road week after week on a succession of gruelling one-night stands, till all peripheral political activities of even the mildest variety become impossible for them to undertake. They arrive in the town, erect the set, act the play, bow to the audience, dismantle the set, load it on to the wagon, fall exhausted into bed, only to scramble the next morning after an objectionably early breakfast into the fug of their minibus for another long grind in some remote and non-comprehending locality, before a public of middle-class art-lovers and sceptical school-teachers who as like as not complain that the play is too *hectoring* and all this left-wing propaganda is losing credibility in this day and age . . .

We discovered that socialist-minded actors of quality committed to placing their art at the service of their politics were more or less unavailable: they had all done their stint for 7:84 in the past and were physically unable to take it any more. Besides, they had families now, and needed domestic permanence: and as their reputations were becoming established, they could get congenial work without much difficulty on TV. So we ended up using 'ordinary' actors with no particular political bent, who were not opposed to 'socialism', and who were prepared to give it a try, after all, it was a job. Some of them were Irish: and were happy to take part in a play about Ireland. Some of them were very doubtful about possible 'pro-terrorist' sentiments in the script. One man refused the part offered him on the ground that he was conscientiously non-violent: and then was next heard of playing in a heavily pro-British Army TV series largely set in Northern Ireland. Irish actors, by the way, are particularly subject to these worries when working in Britain: the Prevention of Terrorism Act is a powerful deterrent to their appearance in anything that dissents from the North of Ireland Office Line, and any hint of 'subversive' associations will do them no good back home either.

At the same time the company itself had to bear in mind the

possible repercussions of too polemical a presentation of the play. In 1977 we had taken part in a conference on left-wing theatre at Oval House in London, where we heard how, for instance, the Red Ladder Company had been unable to get bookings in trade union halls for work that dealt with Ireland. There was also the example of the Recreation Ground group which lost its Arts Council grant after touring a play about Ireland accompanied by serious 'revolutionary-orientated' discussions with the audiences. As we were directing our play, we were ex-officio part of the 7:84 collective structure during rehearsals. We obtained the agreement of the rest of the 'collective' that the decor should include a variety of posters, news-cuttings, and so on, relating to the 1978 situation in Northern Ireland. Also we had handbills on this subject given out to the public as it passed through the foyers. We wanted the play to strengthen the arguments of the Troops Out of Ireland Movement, and to alert people to the dreadful state of affairs in the H Blocks of Long Kesh. We trusted in the political nature of the company to back us up in this.

Once the tour had commenced, however, and we had made those modifications to the production demanded by our experience of the first performances, we were no longer on the payroll as directors. The company on the road was supposed to administer its own affairs from now on, and its collective no longer included us. No sooner had this point been reached — ironically enough, in the west of Ireland — than our posters, news-cuttings and handbills disappeared from human eye. The play thus became a nineteenth-century historical melodrama, put on for its own sake, as it might be Boucicault's *Colleen Bawn* . . . delightful indeed, if you like that kind of thing: but why spoil all the romanticism with so much talk about revolution, and what on earth was that man doing in the Epilogue muttering about 'the red-stained Crown' and 'Republican Brotherhoods' and fouling up all the sentiment of Roisin's pathetic fate? People who didn't see it like that could only discern a bombastic attempt at transferring David Hare's *Fanshen* to an Irish setting and missing out all the gravely-delineated social detail. The play-plus-context as a political activity in itself had been replaced by

a play, *tout court*, that just happened to include some politics in
the plot.

A plot, incidentally, of considerable complexity, which could
only be justified by our need to interlink a number of political
themes (Irish tenants, black slaves, co-operation *v* exploitation,
co-operation *v* sectarian rivalry, revolution *v* reform, feminism,
racialism, predatory sexuality, and so on, with all their
contradictions) against a background of a society at a time of
critical change. The technique we employed is one which we
have always used in our work (both D'Arcy/Arden and Arden
alone). Perhaps because we had been absent from the British
theatre for some years, we did not realise how unused the regular
audiences for 'socialist theatre' were to such a style. 7:84's
productions had commonly involved a fairly straightforward
statement of one main social issue, interspersed with didactic
ballads and dialectical tirades, and rarely getting embrangled
in elaborate constructed fictions full of such traditional devices
as disguises, amatory misunderstandings, last-minute revelations,
and intercepted messages. This did not make for an easy
understanding on the part of audiences — for instance in Ireland
some objections were raised by people who apparently left the
theatre at the end of the first Act, disgusted by what they took
to be a play totally in favour of benevolent paternal landlords
with their efforts blessed by the clergy of both denominations.
That the plot itself could extend to illustrate the irony of this
interpretation did not seem to have occurred to them: this was
not what they had come to expect from 7:84.

The final irony of the production took place in Belfast, when
one of the authors (D'Arcy) arrived at Queen's University, where
the play was part of the annual Festival — a festival overtly
presented to the world as an indication of the 'normality' of
Northern Ireland, an aspect in fact of the British Government's
psyops programme to isolate 'terrorism', reaffirm bourgeois
non-sectarian culture, and diminish any possibility of artistic
folk applying their imaginations to the real normality of the
North, which is one of permanent oppression and resistance.
She had at this time no formal relationship with 7:84: but was

an official guest of the Festival in that she had been invited to
deliver a lecture by the English Department of Queen's. The
subject of her lecture was 'Theatre in an Age of Reform' and
dealt with some of the issues we have already outlined in this
preface. Because our posters etc. were no longer on view, thus
removing as it were the author's voice from the presentation
of her own play; because the Art for Society exhibition in the
Ulster Museum (also a part of the Festival) had been banned
because of the political content of some pictures in it; because
a mass-rally in Armagh about H Block had been banned; because
everyone around the Festival was saying that no-one in Belfast
was interested in H Block (of course they weren't — the activities
were all being banned): and because she had been invited as an
'international artist' to participate in and presumably envigorate
the Festival — she wrote the words H Block on a wall in the
Museum during a Festival poetry-reading, was arrested, and
remanded in custody. Arden delivered her lecture in her place,
in a swirling miasma of excruciating embarrassment from
University and Arts Council personnel responsible for the
Festival. The play continued its allotted run without any
statement made either from the stage or in a programme note
about the whereabouts of one of the authors (Armagh Gaol:
for the next three weeks: experiencing a great deal at first hand
of the Age of Reform in 'normalised' Ulster), and then the
actors went back to Britain to carry on *Vaudaleur's Folly*, leaving
her behind them like Roisin in the last scene of our own Act
Two.

In the spring of 1979 we paid a visit to Greece, where we met
many theatre people. During one of our conversations we spoke
about the role of women in Greek classical theatre, as seen by
modern Greek actresses in the aftermath of the Fascist Colonels'
junta. Women, we were told, practically never had a chance to
play roles of 'power', 'social authority', 'decision-making',
because of the structure of the ancient plays and their
importance in the 20th century repertory. Much the same, we
realised, could be said of Shakespeare in Britain. So long as men
were always cast as gods, tyrants, heroes, the sexual attitudes
that had lain behind the military coup in Greece could only be

reinforced by cultural conventions. If Aeschylus, Sophocles and Euripides had written women's parts for men to play because of the social conditions of their age, why by the same token could not their men's parts in our age be played by women? So many of the Greek actresses are artists of great strength and intensity: and we could so easily see them in such roles as Oedipus or Orestes. Once again the Shakespearian analogy came to mind.

Later on in the same year D'Arcy attended a workshop at an all-day 'Women-in-Entertainment' seminar in London. Here she spoke about what the Greek actresses had told her and put forward the suggestion that male domination of the professional theatre was largely due to the uncritical acceptance of sexual type-casting — that men did not have to play men, as a rule of nature, just as it is not necessary to find a hunchback for Richard III or a dotard for King Lear — that the response of male actors to roles of cruelty, rapacity, violence and military force was extremely equivocal and tended to fortify an unseemly romanticism towards such undesirable social tendencies — and that the 'sexual authority' of even benevolent male roles was unduly strengthened by inevitable male casting. In a society where women's lives are still largely subservient to men's, it is not realistic to expect dramatists to write only idealised portraits of dominant women in order to redress the balance: plays must deal with life *as it is* quite as much as life *as it should be*. But if audiences were to receive the playwrights' pictures of sexual dominance interpreted not by the dominators but by the dominated, could not a new kind of criticism of received attitudes result from what might superficially seem to be merely a new directors' gimmick? This notion went down very well with Women-in-Entertainment: it was instinctively seen to be a vital ingredient in any revision of patriarchal culture in the theatre: and it is to be hoped that a well-argued paper may yet be written on the subject. Be that as it may, as we are playwrights and in control of the destinies of our work (thanks to the hard-fought battles of the Theatre Writers' Union) we propose to place *Vandaleur's Folly* without delay into the Hazard of Experiment.

When this play is performed by a professional company, the male parts are to be played by women.

M. D'A. & J.A.
Corrandulla, Co Galway.
December 1980.

Characters

SINGER

PRESENTER

WILLIAM THOMPSON } *revolutionary*
ANNA WHEELER } *philosophers*

PEASANT GUERRILLAS *'Lady Clare Boys'*

MICHEAL *a small-farmer/fisherman*

ROISIN *Micheal's sister, a servant-girl*

SOLDIERS *of the British Army*

WILBERFORCE *an American slave-
trade agent*

HASTINGS *an estate-steward*

VANDALEUR *a country gentleman*

EMILY *Vandaleur's wife*

ROXANA *an American lady*

SERGEANT *of the British Army*

RECEPTIONIST *at the Shelbourne Hotel*

DOWAGER

MAJOR BAKER-FORTESCUE *an
absentee landlord*

LORD MAYOR *of Dublin*

ARCHBISHOP *of Dublin (Church of
Ireland)*

ROBERT OWEN *philosopher*

LADIES

GENTLEMEN

WAITER *at the Hell Fire Club*

CRAIG *a socialist co-operator*

PEASANTS

HAGAN *a publican*

CATHOLIC PRIEST } *at Ralahine,*
CHURCH OF IRELAND PARSON } *County Clare*

KITTY *Baker-Fortescue's kitchen-maid*

HIGH SHERIFF *of County Clare*

LAWYER

SURGEON

RELATIVES *of William Thompson*

FLANAGAN *a builder*

CHURCH OF IRELAND PARSON *of
    Thompson's parish, County Cork*

CROUPIER *at the Hell Fire Club*

The action of the play takes place in Ireland (County Clare, Dublin and County Cork) between 1831 and 1833. The precise dates of the various events are not closely defined.

Vandaleur's Folly was first performed on tour in 1978 by the 7:84 Theatre Company, with a cast of nine.

PROLOGUE

Prologue

A ship at sea. Storm and stress. THOMPSON *and* ANNA *are on the deck, muffled up against the weather, leaning on the rail and bracing themselves as the vessel heaves.*

To one side of the stage: the PRESENTER. *To the other: a (female)* SINGER.

SINGER (*air: 'Long Lankin'*).
    'It's an old song and a true song as cold as a bone
    That I cannot stop singing till I come into my own.'

PRESENTER (*speaks*):
    Gray storm upon the sea from the rocks of France
    To the roaring tide-race of the Cove of Cork —
    Foul wind tonight for those who strive toward Ireland . . .

SINGER.
    'Till I come to my own in my own Irish land
    An old song and a true song and where is the end?'

THOMPSON. There can be no end before death's end and death comes too soon. I, William Thompson, Revolutionist, Irishman, Socialist, hereditary landowner and therefore a born thief —

ANNA. I, Anna Wheeler, daughter of an Archbishop, acclaimed the Goddess of Reason in the salons of revolutionary France, and a notorious social outcast . . .

ANNA *and* THOMPSON. We return home to our own land —

ANNA. From our wanderings in France we return, among the disappointed voices of the revolutionaries of Europe —

THOMPSON. Desperate seasick from the wanderings of my life, already condemned to the death of my body — the irreversible black cap of judgement stuffed into the blood of my lungs, making black every breath of my polemic — (*He breaks off in a fit of coughing.*)

PRESENTER. What came you into this wilderness to see. . . ?

> An old man broken coming home to his home to die
> Who yet has wealth enough to make his death
> In comfort with his woman like a pasha
> Amid quilts and silks and sensual warm baths,
> And yet can find no comfort because he is
> An Irishman and Revolutionist . . . ?
> What hope to solve the furious contradictions — ?

THOMPSON. The furious contradiction of Ireland is this: the alleged revolutionaries all over Europe believe that the Age of Revolution has given way to the Age of Reform.

ANNA. Call it the age of defeated revolution — like the Americans we rose up against Great Britain for independence from colonialism, like the French we rose up against our cormorant ruling-classes. The British Army broke our back.

THOMPSON. We broke our own back. We had a Parliament, oh a Protestant landlord Parliament, but by God, woman, it was our own: and we sold it to the pimps of London! And once again they all bend and are bent by the bribery of Reform. . .

ANNA. Five million of the dispossessed: there is nobody can bend them.

THOMPSON.
> They were not bent, they were not even broken
> When bold Wolfe Tone in 'ninety-eight was taken,
> Huddled to prison, badgered to his death. Forsaken
> Only, for the time, this multitude, that's all.

ANNA.
> They seem to sleep, turn hungry faces to the wall:
> And yet they dream most dangerously. When they awaken —

VOICES (*all around*). END BRITISH RULE, GET OUT OF IRELAND NOW, TROOPS OUT, BRITS OUT. . . !

PRESENTER.
> Were Marx and Engels crazy when they said:
> No freedom for the English working-class
> Until at last exerted to reverse
> Its base acceptance of Imperial chains
> Wrapped spike and hook and padlock round the flesh,

Divided bloody human meat of Ireland —
Marx, Engels, Connolly — the words of —

The storm noises drown his speech, with the slogan-voices again.

SINGER.

'The cold rain of Ireland blows over the water
To furrow the face of fair England's proud daughter.

How long will it fall, O as sharp as a knife?
Till the dogteeth of England let go of our life.

Let go of our heart and the voice in our throat:
Till the day of that good-morning, no end to the fight. . .'

The storm rises to a climax. They go.

ACT ONE

Act One

Scene One

The Irish Coast. A foggy night. SOLDIERS *with muskets slouch across the stage, patrolling. When they have gone, a few whistling calls: then a group of* PEASANT-GUERRILLAS, *disguised in women's shawls, gather swiftly and silently together. One of them is* MICHEAL. *Another whistling call, offstage.*

MICHEAL. Who's there?

GUERRILLA-LEADER (*off*). Lady Clare.

1ST GUERRILLA. Lady Clare and who else?

GUERRILLA-LEADER (*off*). Lady Clare and her Brave Boys.

The LEADER (*disguised like the others*) *slips in. He holds a bunch of small sticks, one of them shorter than the others. He distributes these, keeping one for himself.*

One, two, three, four, five — six.

They all check their sticks. MICHEAL *has drawn the short one. He stands a little apart from the others.*

(*To* MICHEAL:)
      We do not know who you are.
      But Lady Clare is well aware
      You are her Brave Boy and you will dare.

He gives MICHEAL *a double-barrelled pistol, a powder horn and shot.*

You will wait here till word comes of where he is.

He clasps hands with MICHEAL: *so do the others, and they go, leaving* MICHEAL *alone. He begins to load his pistol: whistles 'The Wearing of the Green' softly to himself. Quick footsteps, off. He starts.*

ROISIN (*off*). Who's there?

MICHEAL. Lady Clare.

ROISIN (*off*). Lady Clare and who else?

MICHEAL. Lady Clare and her Brave Boys.

> ROISIN, *a hunchback, scurries in — he recognizes her with surprise.* MICHEAL *is about to speak but she stops him.*

ROISIN. Ssh. . . I do not know you. If you know who *I* am, you are to keep it to yourself.

MICHEAL. He will be at his house?

ROISIN. He will not. He is on the road. He is on the road to this place. But be careful: there is another man, a stranger, tonight upon the strand. Take care he does not see you — and patrols —

> *Heavy footsteps, off.*

MICHEAL. Patrols — *now* — get out of it — hide — !

> *Some confusion as he scrambles with his pistol-loading business, dropping things.*

ROISIN. No: *you* hide, you damfool — I'm not the one with the gun — !

> *She manages to hustle* MICHEAL *into hiding with his weapon as the* SOLDIERS *enter. They hear the sound and stop, suspicious.*

1ST SOLDIER. Hello there — who's that!

> ROISIN *makes a dash for it, coming out of hiding in a different place from where she thrust* MICHEAL *in.*

2ND SOLDIER. Don't move — stay where you are or I shoot!

1ST SOLDIER. Catch im — !

2ND SOLDIER. Get im that way — !

> *They chase* ROISIN *around the stage, corner her, and pull her shawl off. When they see who she is —*

1ST SOLDIER. Fuckin roll on, look at this.

2ND SOLDIER. D'you call it a bint or a bloody baboon?

They toss her back and forward between the two of them, and laugh at her.

The SOLDIERS *go out. The sound of their footsteps recedes. When they are completely away,* MICHEAL *comes out of his hiding-place. His shawl has slipped off, revealing his face.* ROISIN *recognizes him, and clasps him in her arms.*

MICHEAL (*putting her off*). Are they gone? Name o' God, *you* go! You are not to be here when —

ROISIN. Put the bullet deep into him. So deep into his cruel womb they will never be able to dig for it.

She runs out. MICHEAL *finishes his pistol-loading, whistling as before. He is suddenly aware of another whistling — 'Dixie' — from offstage. He slips into hiding again.* WILBERFORCE *enters, strolls around edgily, lights a cigar, strolls, whistles, looks at his watch.*

WILBERFORCE. Punctilio of the Irish: three-quarters of an hour late. . . where to tarnation is he? (*He calls softly:*) Hastings. . . ? Are you there. . . ? Hastings?

HASTINGS (*offstage, calling softly*). Over here, sir, over here.

WILBERFORCE. Where? Where, I can't see you?

HASTINGS (*offstage*). To the north. Walk to the north.

WILBERFORCE. What kinda location is north in this wilderness? This way?

HASTINGS (*offstage*). No no sir — this way. And don't make so much noise. There are soldiers' patrols on the strand. (*A shot offstage, followed by a scream from* HASTINGS.) Oh God I am killed! Mr Wilberforce, sir, Mr Wilberforce — please — !

A second shot, offstage. HASTINGS' *cries become a sickening gobble.* WILBERFORCE *moves away in horror, backwards.* MICHEAL *runs out from his hiding-place, and bumps into the back of* WILBERFORCE, *tangles with him briefly, losing his shawl as he does so, and runs off.* WILBERFORCE *holds the shawl, but does not seem to notice it.*

WILBERFORCE. That's it. That's it. Finished. (*He runs out.*)

Scene Two

Ralahine House in County Clare. Enter VANDALEUR *fussing with his botany, and* EMILY.

VANDALEUR. All the portions of seed-potato, different heights, different temperatures — a variety of parts of the house, let them germinate. Mrs Vandaleur, would you be so good as to hold this thermometer, *here*. Put a hook in the wall, later. Already a hook for this one, *here*.

EMILY (*holding a thermometer at the height he indicates*). How long, Mr Vandaleur, do you desire me to stand —

VANDALEUR.(*not listening to her*). My correspondent in Wiltshire suggests three or four weeks, but I fancy —

EMILY. What?

VANDALEUR. Hastings, of course, once I can stir him from his natural indolence, will have prepared a manure-bed at the corner of the orchard — where *is* Hastings. . . ? What's that noise. . . ?

ROXANA (*off*). Hi, hello there — anyone at home — ?

VANDALEUR (*as* EMILY *makes a move to see who it is*). No don't move, pray do not open the door, the drop in the temperature —

Enter ROXANA *struggling with a great travelling-trunk.* EMILY *goes to embrace her.*

EMILY. Roxana!

VANDALEUR. No no the thermometer — !

He takes the thermometer and holds it as EMILY *greets* ROXANA.

EMILY. Why, Roxana, here already, what kind of a journey — Mr Vandaleur, my cousin Roxana, from America, you must have remembered her visit? My dear, how did you carry that gargantuan box all the way from the coach? Why didn't you ask for a servant?

VANDALEUR *abstractedly greets* ROXANA *and wanders out*

again, after putting the thermometer back into EMILY's
hand. ROXANA *sits down on the box, and gives an agonised
jerk.*

ROXANA. My dearest Emily, do you *have* servants, the whole
estate seems entirely deserted — oh! My back, I must have
twisted it —

EMILY. Oh dear what are we going to do — I can't move with
this — Roisin, Hannah, Padraic, where are you — ! Roisin!

Enter ROISIN.

Linament, girl, quick!

ROISIN. We were all of us held up, ma'am, with the crowds in
the town after the election.

EMILY. I don't want to hear another word about that dreadful
election. Linament!

ROISIN *goes off to get linament.*

All my family, you know, and Mr Vandaleur's family, such
partisans — on the losing side; and the supporters of O'Connell
have been so fanatical — ssh. . .

ROISIN *comes back with linament and undoes* ROXANA's
clothing to rub her back.

But oh my goodness, how long can you stay, one month at
least, two. . . ? Such excitement, there'll be all the parties,
the balls at the Limerick Assembly, but with the political
trouble, I do wonder if —

ROXANA. I guess this is going to be a mighty disappointment,
but I can't stay a week, let alone a whole month. I have to
go right away to Dublin.

EMILY. Oh my dear. But we understood you would be in County
Clare till the time came for your visit to London. Oh I'd love
to go to Dublin with you, but my husband with his wretched
experiments —

ROXANA. Just before I took ship from New York — in the hotel
— there was this man, I saw him, thank God he didn't see me,
he was booked on another ship, left a day or two earlier direct

for Dublin, Shelbourne Hotel, Dublin, I saw it on his baggage — I have to follow him, find out what he's up to.

EMILY. But my darling — is this *romance* — you have incurred an attraction to a mysterious stranger —

ROXANA. No stranger, no mystery neither. A notorious slave-trader.

EMILY. But the slave-trade is illegal.

ROXANA. Not in America, not in Cuba, which is where this man operates. And the ships in his illegal trade carry sugar back to Europe, and that could be his business here: my father told me, if I find him, follow him up. . . oh!

She has moved and hurt her back again. Business with ROISIN:

No, lower down, honey, rub it there, there, that's it, I'll try to stay still. You've got to appreciate, cousin Emily, when my father's plantation in Carolina went bankrupt, he began a new business in the Northern States. You say — political troubles. . . ? So you know what I mean. Columbia the land of the free is tangled into nightmare by the one issue of negro slavery. . .

Enter VANDALEUR, *rummaging.*

VANDALEUR. A crucial piece of potato left down in that corner, did I put it by error back inside my laboratory — ?

EMILY (*getting between him and* ROXANA's *déshabillé*). Mr Vandaleur, no — you can't come in now — out. . . ! Roisin, the thermometer!

She thrusts the thermometer into ROISIN's *hand as she urges him out of the room.*

A crucial piece of potato. . . ? Under the box! Roisin —

They forget the thermometer and lift first ROXANA, *then the box. The potato is crushed, underneath it.*

ROISIN. Oh ma'am, pulverised — no good to the master at all. . .

EMILY. Get rid of it, hide it —

ROISIN *gets rid of it.* ROXANA, *displaced, finds she can walk about more easily.* EMILY *starts to do up her dress for her.*

So your father expunges his guilt as a repentant slave-owner by sending you all over the world to investigate like a Royal Commission, I declare it's pure tyranny. Ah, the one we should get you to meet is Mrs Wheeler, in County Cork, I say Mrs advisedly, because of course she's not. . . but she can tell you all about it, statistics, everything, absolute horrors out of all the blue-books — she —

SERJEANT (*off*). You that way, you that way, round the back there one man: move!

EMILY. Goodness gracious, what is that?

Enter SERJEANT *and* SOLDIERS.
ROISIN *goes out*.

SERJEANT. You'll excuse me, madam, ladies, I have my duty to perform. You, through the front garden, two potting-sheds and a summer-house, make sure they're clear!

1ST SOLDIER. Serjeant.

The SOLDIERS *crash across the stage and out the other side*.

SERJEANT. What happens through here?

Enter VANDALEUR, *confronting him*.

VANDALEUR. Through here, sir, is my laboratory. Might I ask what you are —

SERJEANT. In accordance with the provisions of the Peace Preservation Act as applicable to County Clare under the military emergency imposed as of yesterday morning, we have instructions to search your property for the perpetrators of last night's outrage. There's the warrant.

He hands VANDALEUR *a document*.

VANDALEUR. Last night's — ?

SERJEANT. Last night's outrage. Of course there's no suggestion, sir, you yourself might be implicated, but we believe the men in question could have taken refuge in your servants' hall. Would you think now that was likely?

Enter ROISIN.

ROISIN (*to* EMILY): Oh madam, madam, and the children so terrified, the poor little lambs. . . !

VANDALEUR (*having read the warrant, nearly collapses*). Oh my God, Emily, help. They have murdered my steward.

EMILY. Mr Hastings?

VANDALEUR. Upon the beach of the estuary. They blew his face away.

SERJEANT. And his belly, sir, his lower belly. Point-blank range. Revolting circumstance.

VANDALEUR. If the murderers are in this house, then of course they must be found. But I cannot believe —

SERJEANT. If we find 'em, you'll have no choice but to believe it, Mr Vandaleur.

EMILY. But Daniel Hastings — why why why? — such a respectable jovial man, and his wife, and his poor children —

SERJEANT. They left a message for his wife, nailed it up to his cottage door. (*He gives* VANDALEUR *a second, dirty, piece of paper.*) Written in blood by the look of it.

(*He calls to the* SOLDIERS *offstage:*) Hey Dobson, Wilkins, if there's nobody in the summer-house, check out them clumps of evergreen, they could hide a whole half-company! Move!

VANDALEUR. Serjeant, you said — emergency. You said — military emergency. What the devil did you mean?

SERJEANT. No more nor what I said, sir. On account of the recent prevalence of agrarian crime, martial law in a manner of speaking has been imposed upon the county by order of the proper authorities. I had assumed you'd have been informed.

(*To the* SOLDIERS *again:*) All right if there's no-one there we'll pack it in and move on down the road. Get fell in on the gravel avenue!

(*He puts his hand out for the dirty paper:*) I'll take that back if you don't mind. Requisite evidence, need to keep it.

VANDALEUR (*dazed*). I — I can't read it, what does it say. . . ?

EMILY. I don't want to look at it. Oh my God that poor woman.

ROXANA (*taking the paper*). May I see? (*She reads:*)
    'Daniel Hastings Number One
    Walked to the strand and never came home
    Who will be next now the work is begun?
    All slave-drivers and informers beware
    Of the vengeance of Lady Clare. . . '

SERJEANT (*taking the paper back*). My advice to you, sir, you should leave home, leave today, don't waste no time. Look after the ladies, that's your duty.

The SERJEANT *goes out.*

VANDALEUR. I believed that my duty was the reform of the rural economy, I believed that a landlord who was absent from his estates was the worst landlord in the whole world. . . Yes: we must go to Dublin. Bring the children. Bring the nursemaid. For the time being, abandon Ralahine. Oh yes: we shall go today.

They go out.

Scene Three

The Shelbourne Hotel, Dublin. A RECEPTIONIST *(male) trying to keep order amongst a throng of excited people struggling with luggage and great cloaks, hats etc. It is clearly foul weather outside. The babel of voices augmented, if there are not enough actors, by taped soundtrack. Among the guests are* VANDALEUR *with* EMILY *and* ROXANA, *and — a little later — a* DOWAGER.

VOICES (*overlapping and sometimes concurrent*). Absolute nonsense you can't let me have a room — would you rather I went home to the west and was murdered in my bed?!
I did write a week ago to bespeak accommodation — is the postal service utterly disrupted by the emergency? —
Good God, man, the chaos in Dublin, playing right into the hands of O'Connell and the Catholics, dammit they *want* us disorganised — But we must have a room, our lives are in danger — we must have a room — we must have a room, we must have a room we must have a room — !

RECEPTIONIST. Ladies and gentlemen, would yous all of yous
listen please! Be *quiet!* (*A sudden hush.*) The Shelbourne Hotel
is well aware of the terrible conditions of disaffection,
revolution, peril to life in the western counties: let me assure
yous all that Dan O'Connell and his crew of hooligans, ladies
and gentlemen, will not be permitted to disrupt the routine of
the Shelbourne Hotel.
Now, sir, you said three bedrooms and a sitting-room for an
entire family, 'tis out of the question. O'Halloran, the
Vandaleur baggage into number thirty-four sharing with
another family, look sharp or they'll have your head off —

VANDALEUR (*to* EMILY): Good heavens, is that all right?

EMILY (*exhausted*). Just take it and be thankful.

The DOWAGER, *forging through, bounces off the reception-
desk and changes course towards* EMILY, *whom she carries
into a corner.*

DOWAGER. Did you say *Vandaleur. . . ?* Good heavens, Emily,
that's not you! Emily *Molony* of County Clare, and what
were you doing, Vandaleur, to protect her from all the
violence? Nothing at all, I suppose, as usual except grafting
your damned gooseberries, impractical as always, improvements improvements and just look where it has led!

VANDALEUR. Ma'am, you will excuse us, my wife is —

DOWAGER. Shattered, of course, *bouleversée,* what else do you
expect —

VANDALEUR *carries* EMILY *off with him, while the*
DOWAGER *retains* ROXANA.

You don't suppose now he's in Dublin, he's going to start his
old habits all over again? More fool her, she should never have
married him, such a spirited girl once —

BAKER-FORTESCUE *has entered and received a letter from
the* RECEPTIONIST. *Before he opens it the* DOWAGER *is
onto him.*

Oh ho ho, Major Baker-Fortescue, ho ho ho my raucous
ravisher — I don't suppose *you're* tempted to resume residence

in County Clare, with every Catholic in the district in arms
like an army of cockroaches — poor Vandaleur, you know,
quite *shattered* by the murderous outrage!

ROXANA *goes out.*

BAKER-FORTESCUE. And why not? Are not all of us? Did you
say he was here? Where is he, I can't see him?

The DOWAGER *surges out:* VANDALEUR *re-enters:* BAKER-
FORTESCUE *confronts him.*

Aha indeed yes, Vandaleur, hello there, come here, sir,
appalling news!

VANDALEUR. Baker-Fortescue, the very man I want to see. This
military emergency —

BAKER-FORTESCUE. The only possible solution. As soon as I
heard of the victory of O'Connell in the County Clare election,
I went straightway to the authorities to demand law and order!
Damme, my dear fellow, I took post upon the doorstep of
Viceregal Lodge like a bully in a brothel-house till that cow's
udder of a Lord Lieutenant was compelled for very shame to
comply. (*He looks around at the noisy throng.*) Five thousand
people if there's twenty — not a man of them dare sleep in
their own beds for months! (*He has unfolded his letter and
finds a printed leaflet.*)

Good God look at this! Rotunda Auditorium, a public lecture
by some bastard called the 'Distinguished Mr Robert Owen',
from England wouldn't you know, upon the 'Advantages
Economic and Social of the Co-operative System of
Agriculture!' Do you go to it?

VANDALEUR. It is tonight?

BAKER-FORTESCUE. It is indeed. Under the patronage of the
Protestant Archbishop and the Lord Mayor of Dublin! Do you
go to it?

VANDALEUR. Long had greatest interest in Mr Owen's most
lucid philosophy, but just now, I don't know, I —

BAKER-FORTESCUE. Oh you must go, you shall, we must all
of us go. It's an obvious Papish trick to soften the gentry in

the face of O'Connellite political obduracy. By the same token, as soon as it's over, I'm making up a small party of a few of our old friends, hearts of oak, bucks and bruisers of the right sort, don't you know, to play the tables at the Hell Fire Club. Do you come?

VANDALEUR. As you know, I do not gamble: and I abhor all games of chance. Our Divine Creator, Fortescue, provided us free will and a reasoning brain that by rational effort alone we might augment opportunity and enlarge our accomplishment.

EMILY *and* ROXANA *re-enter.*

BAKER-FORTESCUE. Oh He did? Perhaps He did. . . At all events, the Rotunda, eight o'clock don't forget!

BAKER-FORTESCUE *suddenly sees* WILBERFORCE, *looking around as though in search of someone. He breaks away from* VANDALEUR *and takes* WILBERFORCE *abruptly into a corner.* EMILY *has come up behind her husband.*

EMILY. The Rotunda? You are going out? Dear me, with the Rapist Fortescue?

VANDALEUR. A learned lecture, Mrs Vandaleur, for economic self-improvement. Do you wish to come too?

EMILY. The children are ill, poor Roisin is unable to cope — my economic self-improvement for this evening will remain domestic. (*She looks at his watch.*) Seven forty-five, you will be late.

VANDALEUR. I shall be late.

VANDALEUR *goes out, calling 'A cab, a cab. . . !'*

EMILY. He surely doesn't hope to catch a cab in this weather — Roxana, what are you staring at?

ROXANA (*who is hiding behind* EMILY, *and watching* WILBERFORCE). Who's that?

EMILY. Major Oliver Baker-Fortescue of His Majesty's Sixth Dragoons — a rural neighbour, when he's at home, which he hardly ever is — we would not call him a friend.

ROXANA. You referred to him as the *rapist*?

EMILY. My dear, he refers to himself so: as a boast: and with truth. In the service of the Crown, but oh yes with truth. Why the interest?

ROXANA. Because the one he is with is my man from New York, that's why. Now what has your military rapist got to do with the Cuban slave-trade?

BAKER-FORTESCUE (*to* WILBERFORCE). What do you mean, County Clare, you were supposed to come *here* to report to *me* first! County Clare is in political turmoil, I will not have you blundering about there all on your own messing everything up!

WILBERFORCE. Major Fortescue —

BAKER-FORTESCUE. *Baker*-Fortescue to you, Wilberforce: I do not relish familiarity.

WILBERFORCE. *Judge* Wilberforce to you, Major. I tell you sir, the political turmoil has already produced enough mess to make you and me reconsider every arrangement we've already made, and the sooner we get it fixed, the safer for both of us.

BAKER-FORTESCUE. Oh very well. But not here. Ten to eight, I'm going to be late. The Hell Fire Club, Mr. Wilberforce — *Judge* Wilberforce, dammit — upon midnight — make sure that you're there. At the card tables as though by accident, don't let them know we know each other. . .

BAKER-FORTESCUE *goes out.* ROXANA *and* EMILY *have crept close enough to hear these last remarks unnoticed.*

WILBERFORCE (*aside as he goes out*). Hail Columbia: and God's own country be the death and doom of decadent aristocrats. . .

WILBERFORCE *goes out.*

ROXANA. I wondered what he'd call himself when he got over this side of the ocean — Wilberforce, sure is appropriate — and *Judge*, too — my God, what a civic conscience. You say this Major Fortescue owns property on the western seaboard of Ireland? They could put slave-ships into the shore there?

EMILY. Slave-ships? All full of black men?

ROXANA. No don't be silly — trade-cargo for Africa for the
purchase of black men — they've to fill up their ships some-
where with a clutter of Birmingham rubbish, they can't load
them in a regular spot because the revenue men have it
embargoed. We have got to find out more!

EMILY. Now you aren't going to try to go to the —

ROXANA. To the Hell Fire Club? Where the hell else? How do
we get there — ?

EMILY. But we don't. It's for gentlemen only. They would
never let us in without —

ROXANA. Without some sort of reason to believe that we were
gentlemen? All the scrimmage of this hotel, we don't know
where they've put our baggage — so —

*She looks quickly around, sees that no-one is looking at them,
and grabs up a couple of large caped men's over-coats that are
lying about nearby. The two women are already wearing
travelling boots under their skirts — they hitch up the skirts
under the long over-coats —*

Now here, my dear, an adventure, you'd never have dreamed
the like in Ralahine, next time that you meet your outrageous
Mrs Wheeler of Cork, you can make her quite blue with
jealousy, I'll bet *she* never dared, anyway. . .

*They clap on a couple of top hats with their hair crammed
underneath — rearrange their scarves to look like men's
cravats — EMILY pins hers in place with her brooch.*

EMILY. Roxana, I cannot believe this — we are the heroine and
her confidante from a nautical melodrama —

She sings (air: 'Polly Perkins of Paddington Green'):
 'Attired in man's raiment
 She bravely set sail
 To fight for sweet liberty
 'Mid gunshot and gale — '

ROXANA (*readjusting* EMILY's *brooch*). No, no, your neck —
let me see — so —

They are now dressed and find themselves face to face with the
RECEPTIONIST.

Shall we go out into the street and take the air, like two
gentlemen?

RECEPTIONIST. Call ye a cab, gentlemen — at the steps of the
door directly — O'Halloran, a cab for these gentlemen — where
to, sir?

ROXANA. The — ah — the Hell Fire Club!

RECEPTIONIST. May ye be favoured at the tables, sir, by the
luck of St Patrick!

ROXANA (*gives him a tip*). And may St Patrick favour you to —
ah — drown the shamrock with this — isn't that right?

The RECEPTIONIST *performs his gratitude ritual and they go.*

Scene Four

The Rotunda Auditorium, Dublin. A large notice announcing
ROBERT OWEN'*s lecture, and a Union Jack at the back of the*
stage. The ARCHBISHOP *and the* LORD MAYOR *take their*
places with OWEN *in between them.* VANDALEUR, BAKER-
FORTESCUE *and some* LADIES *are in the audience.*

LORD MAYOR. Mr Owen, the economic philosopher, well-known
to you all, what more appropriate than a few short words from
His Grace the Archbishop. . .

ARCHBISHOP. My Lord Mayor, such terrible times, the Irish
nation torn in sunder — political sectarian strife. Indication of
our communal will to contest these manifestations, shall we
all of us please rise for the National Anthem. . .

'God Save the King' is played. All rise. THOMPSON *and*
ANNA *enter through the audience. He has a French tri-colour*
at the end of his walking-stick, she has a red cap of liberty with
a tri-colour cockade and a tri-colour sash. They sit down
pointedly facing the audience below the platform. The anthem
ends, everyone else sits: the ARCHBISHOP *rises again.*

ARCHBISHOP. My lords, ladies, and gentlemen, desperate
violence, assassinations, one hundred and ninety-six motiveless
murders within the space of twelve months. For the social
amelioration to be propounded by Mr Owen, enormous hopes
of all persons of good will in the community —

ANNA. As the daughter of an Archbishop, may I point out to
the Archbishop that the motiveless murders are largely
provoked by the system of tithes, whereby the Roman
Catholics are compelled by law to contribute to the coffers
of an alien church, the Archbishop's own Protestant Church — ?

THOMPSON. You not only cause terrorism by your annual
income, Archbishop, but when terrorism is extirpated, you
must do without your port-wine.

Cries of anger from BAKER-FORTESCUE *and the* LADIES.

If the Lord Mayor will take into account the blatant failure
of the London Government to give Catholics the legal ability
to hold seats in the House of Commons, this meeting could
prove constructive.

ANNA. No payment of tithes without representation!

LORD MAYOR (*rising*). Myself a whole-hearted advocate of
Parliamentary reform —

BAKER-FORTESCUE (*from the floor*). Let the Papists into
Parliament, they will crush the Protestant community — but
the Loyal Orange Order will never —

LORD MAYOR. The brilliant Mr O'Connell, I happen to know,
is totally loyal to the British Crown —

BAKER-FORTESCUE. The loyalty of O'Connell, sir, directed
solely to his bank-balance —

ANNA. Are we talking about the stock exchange or pitch-and-
toss at Donnybrook Fair?

BAKER-FORTESCUE. I will not bandy arguments with a female
dressed-up as poll-parrot! Can lead only to a repetition of
the Jacobin rebellion of 1798.

LORD MAYOR. Mr O'Connell the staunchest opponent of the
egalitarians of '98 —

BAKER-FORTESCUE. A mere cloak to cover over his subversive intent to break the link with Great Britain!

THOMPSON. But what harm, sir, to the British, if we did break the link?

BAKER-FORTESCUE. Good God, you do not *advocate* republican separatism! A separated Ireland is a permanent military threat to the integrity of British democracy, and I speak as a professional soldier.

THOMPSON. I don't think the Americans —

BAKER-FORTESCUE. I don't want to hear about America — the Americans are like the French, they stretch out for Empire everywhere, the West Indies alone —

ANNA. You have an interest in the West Indies?

BAKER-FORTESCUE. Madam, never you mind where I have an interest —

THOMPSON. International financial manipulation, is that it, ho? How many bribes were paid to Protestants in shape of Empire Free Trade to secure the Act of Union? How much are you paid to beat your sectarian drum by the likes of the Duke of Cumberland and the rest of the English Tories?

BAKER-FORTESCUE. The English Tories at least will preserve our Protestant liberty!

THOMPSON. Did not your Protestants in the seventeenth century chop off the King's head? Dear sir, if you're a logical Protestant, you will also be a Jacobin —

ANNA. Once you start dispossessing the mighty of their seats, Major Charlotte Corday Fortescue, who can tell you where it will stop!

BAKER-FORTESCUE (*in a baffled frenzy*). Ho ho the female revolution, hen treading cock arsey-versey — cock-a-doodle-doo, cock-a-doodle-doo, papa papa I have laid an egg. . . !

LADIES (*joining in at the same time*). Bitch — virago — go back to your husband, (*etc., etc. . .*)

BAKER-FORTESCUE. They should fuck the likes of her upon

all fours like the animal she is — cock-a-doodle-doo —

He seizes the Union Jack and flaps it in THOMPSON's *face.*

THOMPSON (*stands on his chair and holds up his tri-colour*).
England observe: when the Irishmen run mad,
Now is your chance to take from them all they had.

ANNA (*on her chair too*).
England beware: when the Irish are quiet and cool,
If you do not stir them up, they will take back from you all
you stole.

Comparative quiet is restored by the LORD MAYOR *and his gavel.*

LORD MAYOR. Mr Owen, Mr Owen, Mr Owen has not yet been heard. . . !

OWEN (*rising, as the meeting subsides*). Your political national problems amount to no more than wrangling over great bags of bandits' booty. The intransigent attitude of each partisan in these disputes is the product of the environment in which he or she willy-nilly has grown up toward stunted maturity. Instead of competition, the ravening hunger of the deepsea shark, I offer you the benefits of Socialist co-operation — whereby every individual should endeavour to put forth the same active exertions to make each other happy and comfortable as they have hitherto done to make each other miserable. Allow your work-people to receive full-fold the fruits of their joint labour, let their elected representatives confer with yourselves upon boards of management, assist actively to determine all projects of self-improvement — and above all let them share equally in the profits of all your enterprise. You will say — "But where do we start. . . ?" —

VANDALEUR (*starting up in the audience*). Mr Owen, sir, excuse me. In County Clare already a start has been made. Immediately before the recent outbreak of terrorism, a large number of our resident gentlemen got together and agreed that the selfishness of the landowners was largely to blame for the disaffection of the rural poor.

OWEN. Very good, sir, excellent, indeed — may I suggest: one small estate, only one out of the whole country, to be at once and without reservation, developed by its enlightened proprietor under form of a co-operative — it would infallibly succeed, and be seen to succeed: and another would immediately follow, and another — till within five years the whole of Ireland could be operating, nay, flourishing, as a congenially-supportive, fully-Socialist commercial structure! What need then of terrorism, what need of these states of emergency, what need of the Orange Order or even of Dan O'Connell within a commonwealth so harmonious. . . !

ANNA. *Utopia redivivus sub manibus dominorum magistrorum episcoporum* — behold a miracle. . . !

THOMPSON. Co-operation from above, extended to the people by the idealism of their controllers — Owen, you're a good fellow, but a fundamental blockhead: for what motive should great men deprive themselves of their only reason for being called great?

BAKER-FORTESCUE. Has every man in this room gone mad. . . ? Co-operation, do you call it that this — this — *speaker* is prating about? There's only one word for *your* word. . . REVOLUTION: and my God, an Archbishop under your armpit as you preach it to us, a Lord Mayor in his golden chain. . . .

THOMPSON. Astonishing the rapidity with which Major Fortescue agrees with me.

ANNA. Only one word for your word indeed and it's my word too.

THOMPSON. I did hope, this evening, Owen, it might in truth have become *yours,* but you speak as you always did, to the wrong crowd and there's no remedy.

VANDALEUR (*running forward*). Ah no, my dear Thompson, you think *that* — you are in error! Mr Owen, how many times has the co-operative system been tried?

OWEN. In Scotland, America, Scotland again, at least according to *my* principles. I have a pamphlet to indicate at some length the lessons to be derived from the mistakes we might be thought to have made —

VANDALEUR. Effectively, though, not yet a complete success?

OWEN. Ah, but I would emphasise —

VANDALEUR. No no, sir, no excuses — I am a scientific man
and I well understand the hazard of experiment. Mr Owen,
I am prepared to place my own fortune in such hazard. I
have endeavoured for many years to run my rural estate
upon the most enlightened and approved modern methods —
not so much with no success, I would say rather abysmal
failure. Culminating this month in the murder of my steward.
Philosophical agriculture applied only to the soil, to the live-
stock, the crops, is quite useless in this country. The social
patterns of the human being at work upon that soil are the
very first specimens we must transfer to our laboratory —
because I did not do that, because I observed my farm
prosperous with the high price of corn in England, and
omitted to examine the *non*—prosperity of my work-people,
I have reaped a most blighted harvest. No: I am decided —
Ralahine shall be co-operative!

Applause. THOMPSON *and* ANNA *shake him warmly by the
hand.*

As I say, my steward is dead: by my own culpable neglect,
short-sightedness, dead. I would be grateful if you could
recommend me some person to take his place,
well-experienced in your theoretical principles.

OWEN. My dear sir, I can most certainly. My most hearty
congratulations: our first convert in Ireland!

More applause. He shakes VANDALEUR's *hand.*

There is one name immediately comes to mind — Mr Edward
Craig at present in Manchester —

VANDALEUR. I will trouble you for his address, I must see him
at once, go to Manchester at once, oh yes yes yes, there is
no time to be lost. . . !

BAKER-FORTESCUE (*as* VANDALEUR, OWEN, THOMPSON
and others confer). When this news is heard in England, there
will be cotton-mills and coal-mines set on fire by Luddite mobs
from Newcastle to Stoke-on-Trent! God forgive you,

Archbishop, for you know not what you do! Whosoever in this room has felt the truth of my discourse in the thick of his entrail, you can meet me at the Hell Fire Club — I shall have a proposition for all right-minded Britons of good spirit and no womanish scruples. . . .

They go out, generally.

Scene Five

The Hell Fire Club, Dublin. ROXANA *and* EMILY, *dressed as men, enter and are conducted towards the card-tables by a* WAITER. *There are* GENTLEMEN *playing cards, drinking, singing; maybe later, dancing. The atmosphere is boozy and ribald but not yet really wild.* BAKER-FORTESCUE *and* 1ST GENTLEMAN *come confidentially to the front of the stage.* WILBERFORCE *is among the company at the back.*

1ST GENTLEMAN. Your information, I'm afraid, Oliver, was only too correct — the liberal faction in the Commons are determined to force through the Bill for Parliamentary Reform: moreover there is no hope whatever for renewed legislation against the trade-unions. . . By the end of next year, a guillotine in St James's Park! How long can the King live? His opposition to Reform is feeble enough, God knows, but at least it does signify. When he dies —

BAKER-FORTESCUE. The eventual heir to the throne a virgin schoolgirl straight from the cradle, under the tits of a liberal wetnurse, to control the British Empire. . . Did you speak to the Duke of Cumberland?

1ST GENTLEMAN. He wants you to be responsible for the activation of the Orange Lodges throughout all the regiments in Ireland.

BAJER-FORTESCUE. No difficulty there. He will himself be making sure of the troops in England.

1ST GENTLEMAN. But when, Oliver, when? We cannot let it hang fire for ever!

BAKER-FORTESCUE. If Princess Victoria is to be deprived of
the succession, and the patriot Duke to become King in her
place, and if we all do what's expected of us our military *coup
d'état* can be ready to be sprung by the end of next year. Go
to the tables, enjoy yourself, we've been in the corner long
enough. . . .

1ST GENTLEMAN *goes to the card-table.* BAKER-FORTESCUE
catches WILBERFORCE's *eye and moves across the stage as
though drunk. They engineer a collision.* EMILY *sees this and
draws it to the attention of* ROXANA. *The two women creep
up to hear the conversation, but the men move about and
they only hear those passages enclosed in square brackets.*

BAKER-FORTESCUE. Dammit, man, you're drunk, do you
propel yourself into me, sir?

WILBERFORCE. Make it appear we have a quarrel. . . ?

BAKER-FORTESCUE. [Perhaps we have. I instructed you to find
a way to make confidential secure arrangements for the loading
of my cargo at the most convenient secret place in or around
the Shannon Estuary: I did *not* want you doing anything
within ten miles of Fortescue Grange:] you have been pouring
out my stinking bath-water on my own front-garden-path, you
bloody fool!

WILBERFORCE. Keep it courteous, between gentlemen, between
partners, I am *not* repeat not your hired man, Major Fortescue,
okay. . . ? [My concern in this business is to oversee financial
arrangements, to hire and fire correct executives. As soon as
you wrote me that your brig 'Maria Edgeworth' was now
known as a suspected slaver — I came right away to the River
Shannon to mosey out the land. So my report, when I made
it to you, would have the advantage of precognition, okay. . .?
So what did I find? Tidal mudflats, you didn't tell me about.
A low-lying coast-line with precious few highways of access,
you didn't tell me about.] So we got to have a man who
knows the tides and the shallows and the hiding-places
inshore like he knows the intimate pimples in the concavities
of his own wife. So I find me such a man: and he sets me up
a surefire deal, and —

BAKER-FORTESCUE. And in the very middle of your surefire deal your 'correct executive' gets himself *shot*. . . . ! God in heaven, Daniel Hastings. . .

WILBERFORCE. Political complications of your Irish aristocracy and their naturally obnoxious lackeys ain't none o' my business. I'm a republican.

BAKER-FORTESCUE. So we now have a stranded cargo, in and around the shores of Shannon —

WILBERFORCE. Cached away safe and sound, Major, in the ruins of an an-tique monastery.

BAKER-FORTESCUE. But the ship, the ship, where is the ship — ?

WILBERFORCE. Gone up the coast standing for orders on and off the port of Sligo. Just as soon as we can locate a replacement for Hastings, we call her back and she loads up. Guess your West Indian investments can hold off their foreclosure another few weeks. . . ?

BAKER-FORTESCUE. That's what *you* think. . . But Goddammit, that monastery is on Ralahine land, don't you realise John Scott Vandaleur has given over all of Ralahine to the blood-enemies of Church and King!

WILBERFORCE. Economic and social complications of Ireland none o' my business. . . .

BAKER-FORTESCUE. And yet. . . why not Ralahine. . . ? By God, it will work two ways! Either my slave-venture, my investment will be secured by the transaction: or else it will be discovered, Vandaleur will get the blame, his thieves-kitchen co-operative discredited for ever. . . ! Why, Judge, I'm a bloody genius — if Napoleon Bonaparte had known about me, he'd have shat in his cocked hat all the way home to Corsica!

He has been drinking steadily and now becomes uproarious. The room in general is becoming uproarious, and the GENTLEMEN *are beginning a degree of brutal horseplay.* BAKER-FORTESCUE *suddenly finds himself confronting* ROXANA *and* EMILY.

Are there one of 'em or two? I'm too drunk to deal with two of 'em. But what a lovely little gentleman, how soft and sweet the curve of his neck. . . You are a stranger in this place, sir? To our Hibernian hospitality? And so are you? (*He sways from* ROXANA *towards* EMILY, *and fingers the brooch at her neck.*) Where d'you come from, that you wear soup-plates of silver-gilt at your Adam's apple? Hungarians, or what are you?

EMILY (*very nervous, but rising to the occasion*). Ce que je me demande c'est pourquoi la plume de ma tante se trouve dans les pantalons de Monsieur le Curé —

BAKER-FORTESCUE. Scrotum o' the Pope, no games to be played with no fucking Frenchmen.

ROXANA. I'm not French: and I do calculate, sir, from my accent you'll deduce my regular domicile? The name is Van Leyden, Jedediah Van Leyden Junior of —

WILBERFORCE (*staring hard at her*). Boston, Massachusetts.

ROXANA. No sir. Philadelphia.

BAKER-FORTESCUE. You are aware of this gentleman's name?

WILBERFORCE. No, Major, not his name.

BAKER-FORTESCUE. Well, I am: he's just told it me. We have Hibernian hospitality — the grand tour of Europe for the young pups of Harvard College, am I right, boy, that's what you're doing here? So leave him alone, he's mine. Your place is the mudflats of the Estuary of Shannon: you go there. . . .

WILBERFORCE *grins ominously and moves away, trying in vain to get close to* EMILY. BAKER-FORTESCUE *pours* ROXANA *a drink and puts his arm round her.* GENTLEMEN *are now firing pistols and smashing things.*

Philadelphia: brotherly love: what they call it pacificism — ?

ROXANA (*letting herself go in a sort of frontier fantasy*). Sir, I had instruction in marksmanship from the younger brother of Daniel Boone. Put a bullet in the right eye of a grizzly-bear at five hundred paces, there ain't nobody can whup me Jedediah Van Leyden Junior between Pittsburgh and Vicksburgh and the mountain-lions o' Newark New Jersey. . . !

She borrows his pistols and indulges in a variety of extravagant feats, to the roaring delight of the company.

BAKER-FORTESCUE. God, a strong horse-pistol in first the left hand then the right, can stand fire and give fire like a true-hearted young buck! And we should all of us take example. . .

They all calm down and gather round him. His tone becomes low, ominous.

You don't need me to tell you civil war like a dead dog is buzzing with flies at every road's-end just the same as ninety-eight. Gentlemen, this poor country is a rotten bog of seditious conspiracy, we are all about to sink.

2ND GENTLEMAN. The only cure for agrarian terrorism is —

BAKER-FORTESCUE. The only cure that the leaders of our Protestant community are apparently aware of is to deliver over everything into the hands of the damned underdog. Every morsel of prosperity that our forefathers erected here by their courage and endurance to be surrendered like a bowl of pigswill to all those who would have prevented us even setting foot on the shores of Ireland! Thirty years ago in the rebellion we stood up for our own and prevailed. And the reason we could do so, was, by God, that we acted first! In the autumn of '97 I took part in the Dragooning of Ulster. Armed horse-soldiers like reaping-hooks into every village, every townland, Catholic, Protestant; who cared? Sword, fire, the cat-o-nine-tails — we spread the women in the mud under us, had the men and the brats watch while we put ourselves through them by troop and platoon. When the rebellion did break, the following year, three-quarters of all Ulster lay as silent as — not quite silent. . . now and then they moaned and groaned. The French, when they landed, found very few friends. The Rapist Fortescue had done his work. Jesus Christ I want a vomit. . . We do the same thing in Clare. But this time, unofficial. The Lord Lieutenant, the High Sheriff, are men of a different kidney: they lie in their own crap in their own beds and they mean to die there. They have forgotten there are still some of us with the old Orange spirit — we'll go to Clare, we'll prove it, and we'll live! I will reopen Fortescue Grange, and from the

portals of my ancient home we will ride to defy and to utterly
ruin the O'Connellites, the midnight murderers, the — the —
vomit again — the co-co-operators and Jacobin socialists.
Order the horses: we leave tonight.

See the look of him there:
So childish-ignorant, so wise. . .

How would you, boy, like Ireland to throw truly wide open
    your eyes,
Dabble blood upon the curls of your soft smooth beautiful
    hair?
Hey, what, boy, do you dare
Make mincemeat out of murderers in the beautiful green
    soft county of Clare. . . ?

You've got a horse? Then we'll get you a horse. Gentlemen,
your last bottle, your last vomit, your last leak into the
fireplace — the sun has already risen, we are on the road in
twenty minutes!

He starts a song, which the GENTLEMEN *all join in.* (*Air:
'Lillibullero'*):
  'Out on the road in the wind and the rain
  We know what we want and we have it and hold
  Rake it and break it and take it again
  Let nobody tell you we're bought and we're sold!
  Slitter slaughter holy water
  Scatter the papishes every one
  Lillibullero lillibullero
  Finish it ever before it's begun. . . !'

EMILY (*aside to* ROXANA *while the song is being sung*). Roxana,
you're not going to —

ROXANA. The closer I stick to him the closer we will hold him
when all the evidence is complete — no, you must keep out
of it, stay with your family, keep alive for my messages, and
for God's sake be there when you're needed for God's sake. . .

BAKER-FORTESCUE (*pulls* ROXANA *away, speaks to* EMILY
en passant): Wear your soup-plate over your bollocks, Frog,
you might want it to protect you from a good solid Hibernian
boot!

All the GENTLEMEN *go out with* ROXANA *and* BAKER-
FORTESCUE *in their midst, the song still continuing.*
WILBERFORCE *watches them off.*

WILBERFORCE (*sings — air: 'O Susanna'*):
  'Soho my pretty Yankee boy, does the wind set fair that way?
  He runs you off to County Clare to run and sport and play,
  To sport and run and fire his gun with his arm around your
    waist,
  Oh pretty Philadelphia boy, where have I seen that face. . . ?'

WILBERFORCE *goes out. As he goes out he sees* EMILY *and
makes a move towards her — she sees him and dodges out of
sight.*

Scene Six

The Shelbourne Hotel, Dublin. Enter VANDALEUR, *followed
by* ROISIN.

VANDALEUR (*sings — air: 'The Boys of Wexford'*):
  'For Manchester with no delay
  To seek and find at last — '

Coat — shawl —

ROISIN *equips him for his journey.*

  'The gambler's throw turned upside down
  The whole of a lifetime past — '

Carpet-bag —

  'I never lived but what I could — '

Umbrella umbrella I want my umbrella —

  'This way and that change course:
  With no delay John Vandaleur
  For Manchester sets forth. . . !'

You give that to your mistress — where the deuce is she, she
never disappears in Ralahine. . . (*He hands* ROISIN *a letter.*)
And this — (*He gives her an abrupt kiss on the forehead.*)
Good-bye.

VANDALEUR *goes. Enter* EMILY, *re-establishing her female clothes.*

EMILY. Doesn't she know that Baker-Fortescue is called what they call him because he *does*? Oh, cousin, you *do* know, you crafty colonial, oh that's why you have me out of it in the very heat of the apprehension. . .

ROISIN. Excuse me, ma'am, the master, he's gone, ma'am, he left this letter.

EMILY (*tearing open the letter*). Oh dear God, Manchester. By the night boat and I have missed him.
    (*Sings — air: 'Laredo'*):
      'Oh why do I stand here unable to handle
      Irresponsible people now this way now that?
      I want and I need to take part in the drama:
      Each time I make an entrance they tell me 'not yet!''

Oh Roisin there's a child crying, go and see to him, go on, girl, irresponsible, hurry — !

They go out.

Scene Seven

The Ralahine Estate. Enter CRAIG.

CRAIG. As a young lad I crouched appalled beneath the horse-hoofs and swinging sabres upon the cobble-stones of Peterloo. . . The whole of my life in Manchester, violence, deprivation, immeasurable squalor: but when I came into County Clare it was as though I had travelled from the bright fields of Eden to the Slough of Despond. Clustered like lice into their rat-ridden cabins, enthralled with disease and the blank apathy of congenital vice — have you ever seen a faction-fight? Debased gentlemen of the countryside stand grinning between two mountains while their ignorant tenants will beat each other's brains out — and the gentlemen themselves from their stronghold of Fortescue Grange lay waste their own lands in an orgy of terrified revenge — and if they don't do it, the soldiers do it. To be frank, I have despaired.

Some PEASANTS *are hanging around. One of them throws a stone.*

My grandfather was a Gaelic Highlander, brandished his clay-more for Bonnie Prince Charlie: but all they can see of me, I'm an Englishman fetched over for the *improvement* of Ralahine — don't that tell you the dead depth of the whole cruel business? *Improvement* is the word here for nowt less than mortal hatred. Means eviction, risen rents, means forced export of miserable emigrants by the shipload to America — and that's me, that's my significance. . . (*He takes a scrawled paper out of his pocket.*) Not only stones. They laid this upon the doorstep of my cottage for me to find. Aye, it's a coffin: and no metaphor. 'Beware the vengeance of Lady Clare.' Of course there are now and then smiling faces to be met on the way — but the implications of those smiles. . . ?

1ST PEASANT *passes, raises his hat politely.*

1ST PEASANT (*in Irish*): Go to the devil. *

CRAIG (*pleasantly also — imitating the phrase in Irish as well as he can*): Go to the devil my good fellow.

Enter VANDALEUR.

VANDALEUR. Ah, Craig, good morning. A spot of trouble with Paddy Murphy?

CRAIG. Trouble? By no means. Why?

VANDALEUR. Heard you telling him to go to the devil — I presumed —

CRAIG. I said nothing of the sort, sir. He said to me good-morning, I said to him —

VANDALEUR. 'Go to the devil.' Your instruction in the Irish language from these people — a little mischievous, misleading, they will have their joke.

CRAIG. Oh, joke, Mr Vandaleur, yes: is this a joke?

He shows VANDALEUR *the picture of the coffin.*

VANDALEUR. Ah. On your doorstep? Ah yes. . .

---

* *Go to the devil*: Teigh don diabhal.
  Approximate pronounciation: 'Chay don jowel'.

CRAIG.
>Daniel Hastings Number One
>Neddy Craig Number Two now the work has begun. . . '

You let me think Mr Hastings died suddenly in the midst of his duty. But he didn't, I have been *told* how Mr Hastings came to his end. What I've not been told is why.

VANDALEUR. I am said by many to be a good landlord: the fact is proved by the fact that I went to Manchester to fetch you over to help me to become a good landlord. I will confess this is all nonsense. I've been a damnably bad landlord: and for one reason, cardinal, the very worst reason of all: I had no notion, Mr Craig, of what my steward Daniel Hastings was up to. I knew what rents he paid me on behalf of the tenants: I never sought to find out what rents they had paid him. I will confess, Mr Craig, that —

CRAIG. Nay don't confess, we're not Papists. Give me reasons instead why I should bide another minute on this God-forsaken turf! You've put me and my good wife into fearful danger, Mr Vandaleur, bringing me over here to replace that scoundrel! I am not going to get killed for the crooked tyranny of Daniel Hastings, nor for your weakness neither in allowing him to carry it on.

VANDALEUR. But Mr Craig, you have *not* replaced him! You are not here as my steward: but to organize a co-operative.

CRAIG. Aye but have you told that to the folk, and if you have, did they comprehend it? You and I, at length, in private, have discussed our plans for this co-operative: now or never make them public. Find out who is opposed to it: and for what reason they are opposed. Mr Vandaleur: it's the last chance: either we take it or I go home.

>He heard me: and the bell was rung beside the stable wall.
>Into the yard they crowded one and all —

A bell rings and the PEASANTS *assemble.*

>He briefly told them what he had in mind
>And who I was and why they would not find
>That Daniel Hastings was alive once more.

VANDALEUR.
> No stewards in the co-operative, no middle-men, but a power
> From all the people, by election, to control and plan
> The work, the wages, and the wealth of Ralahine.
> Rules, we shall have, they have been written out,
> A constitution, ratified by vote,
> Committees, trustees, an universal voice
> By which you all can prove the virtue of your choice.

MICHEAL. If you please, sir, the poor people, sir, who do not
have the English — will I put what you have said into Irish for
them before you go on?

CRAIG. What he said to them in Irish took twice as long as in
English, twice as long, three times as passionate, and the same
question flung out from the crowd over and over —

PEASANTS (*one after another abruptly, in Irish*): *What about
the Englishman, what is he doing here?* *

MICHEAL. There is a question, Mr Vandaleur, from some of the
rural people, d'you see what I mean, on the matter of the
guarantees. The new English gentleman, sir, are we guaranteed,
Mr Vandaleur: he will understand the misunderstanding some
of the lads was after having with Mr Hastings, when he was alive?

CRAIG.
> I myself made it clear
> I did not want to hear
> Neither for good nor for bad
> About Daniel Hastings finished and dead.
> I myself made it clear
> There was nothing they need fear —
> My own name would be put forward to the hazard of the vote:
> If they did not want me, then by God I should get out —
> If they agreed that I should stay
> I would work here every day
> Upon equal terms the same as they —

---

* *What about the Englishman, what is he doing here?*: Céard faoi an
Sasanach, céard a ndéanaigh sé annseo?
Approximate pronounciation: 'Caird fwee on sashna, caird-a-nuneena
shay onsha?'

> To advise but not command
> The administration of the land
> And the people and the livestock and the tillage
> And the building of the new most salubrious model village
> Mr Vandaleur and I had planned —
> The sanitary cottages, the school, the public hall.
> The public voice, the public vote, supreme above it all.

Once again put into Irish, they considered it in Irish, looked at me, looked at each other, I looked hard at the strange young man who had taken it upon him to interpret.

PEASANTS (*growling dubiously in Irish*): *What about the rent. . .?*

MICHEAL. They had a most hard question for the master: I put it to him — if we are all in the co-operative, sir, and we all vote together for ourselves, to whom and how much do we pay rent?

VANDALEUR. The Ralahine Co-operative Association as a body, that is yourselves, self-determined, will pay rent as a total body, in form of produce. Of course, guarantees for your security under the arrangement. In a sense I shall pay my own rent from myself *ex-officio* President of the Association to myself as Proprietor of the land. By the same token, no individual liability for the iniquitous tithe. The whole of that is taken care of, under guarantee, by me.

> Nothing else I could have said
> Would have hurled up their hats so high
> So fast from every head. . . !

The PEASANTS *cheer.*

MICHEAL. And for the vote — I told them in Irish they had all marched to support the vote for O'Connell, when not one of them themselves was qualified for a vote, not being freeholders nor even leaseholders but the poor slaves of Ralahine — and yet now, within Ralahine, there was all of a sudden a vote — what they call beyond in England the *universal suffrage* which not even in England have they got! And here it

---

* *What about the rent. . . ?*: Céard faoi an cíos. . . ?
  Approximate pronounciation: 'Caird fwee on shoss. . . ?'

was given to them: so I told them they should take it.

CRAIG. And they did. They elected me amongst them as a
member of the co-operative. There was some question,
wrangled over in Irish, that the proposed rent would be too
great. I made it clear, through the interpreter, that control of
the production in the hands of the Committee would ensure
that once the rent, already fixed, had been paid, the remaining
surplus, and indeed growth of surplus, would be entirely at
their own disposal: and this contented them.

Mr Vandaleur, at this point, with his own hand had written down
His own personal regulation, as a *sine-qua-non*. . .

VANDALEUR. Gambling, alcoholic drinking, opprobious
nicknames will be totally forbidden in the Ralahine Co-operative.
They are all of them symptomatic of the most corrosive
degraded envy: the competitive envious spirit is the first thing
to be banished from the bounds of our new community. Is
that clear?

MICHEAL. Clear enough, it gave small pleasure: the worst to be
hurt by it — Cornelius Hagan, who had the shop, the public
house, the grip of the usurous gombeen upon everyone of us
there — he made a point not to speak the Irish. . .

HAGAN (*pushing forward*). The only vote that we need is the
Catholic vote in Parliament: O'Connell alone can provide it:
O'Connell alone can secure the good word of the Pope for
deliberations and associations so Holy Ireland once again can
come truly into her own.

MICHEAL. They knew him for what he was. They voted him out.

HAGAN *goes*.

(*Sings — air: 'What would you do if you married a soldier?'*):
'Will we patch up our quarrels or will we be fighting
Or can it be worse than ever it was
We've never a hope if we do not try something
Ride on a cow if we can't find a horse.'

To the people, in Irish, I said one thing more: Lady Clare
and her Brave Boys are neither dead nor departed from
Ralahine. We have heard guarantees. Lady Clare will be

walking wide-awake every night to make sure they are held to: so long as they are held to she will not be seen. The print of her feet nonetheless in the morning dew. . . So why not dance. . . ?

ROISIN (*sings, as they all dance*):
    'I looked to me mother I looked to me father
    I looked to the holy man high on the hill
    And never a word from the one to the other
    But "Do what ye have to do, then come and tell". . . '

CHORUS (*sung as they dance*).
    'A rout the da dee, the dum diddly da dum
    A rout the da, doubt the da, diddly da dum
    Da da diddly da dum
    Da dee da dum da diddly da dee da diddly da dum. . . '

The PRIEST *and the* PARSON *have entered and stand in an attitude of formal benediction.*

PRIEST.
    God's blessing on the work, my friends —

PARSON.
    Rebellion, and revolt, now ends
    Forever on this day in Ralahine.

CRAIG.
    And all at last that needed to be done was done:
    The Papist and the Protestant had both joined in the fun.

They go, with cheers and more dancing.

Scene Eight

Fortescue Grange. Enter ROXANA, *dressed as a man.*

ROXANA. Month after month everywhere, even over the water to England, and then back again to Clare, thank God so much of the time I was free and clear from this Fortescue Grange, and its crew of debased gentlemen.

    She sings: (Air: 'George Collins'):
    'They ride out by day and they ride beneath the moon
    The green fields bleed and groan —

If a ragged slave of Ireland came crying to me for help
I must show him a face of stone.

Be free, be free, poor Christian, I would say,
Be free by your own angry hand:
For what have I to do with a white man's broken life
When my mind is in the black man's land. . . ?'

At last, this afternoon, it has been there to some purpose. In the dense rhododendrons under the ever-shuttered windows of the dark house of Fortescue, I have found Wilberforce has fixed himself an exclusive secret meeting. Here he comes.

ROXANA *conceals herself as* WILBERFORCE *enters, lights a cigar, walks about whistling 'Dixie'. Enter* MICHEAL, *whistling 'The Wearing of the Green'. They wander about covertly for a while, then become aware of each other.*

MICHEAL. The man beyond was after telling me that the foreign gentleman, meaning you, sir, had been concerned to have the word out for a good man with the share of a boat and an acquaintance with the tides of the river. I could put the word out for one of the Ralahine boys meself, sir: with the new co-operative, there's great work to be done there at Mr Vandaleur's lobster-pots, would give grand opportunity for the feller that's accorded the charge of it. 'Tis the matter however of the right price for the work. The young feller I have in mind, sir —

WILBERFORCE. Accorded the organizing of the Vandaleur lobster-pots? Tarnation take it, man, my Havana ceegar is swirling smoke under his nostrils this minute. How much?

MICHEAL. When you blew that same ceegar into the long nose of Daniel Hastings, he had information well enough there was a crowd of coal-black niggers to cure and roll the baccy. To my mind that's more than the smuggling of brandy: the devil of a high price in it, 'twould be the gallows for the lad that goes wrong.

WILBERFORCE. Just you name it, we'll agree. . .

MICHEAL. And the month, sir, the day of the month? Dark nights and high enough water don't come all that often together.

WILBERFORCE. We'll let you know. Just name your price.

MICHEAL. I'll put the word out. I'll let you know.

WILBERFORCE *and* MICHEAL *go out.*

ROXANA (*emerging*). My God, Ralahine, and a slave-dealer's
garter-snake in the very middle of the new co-operative! I
have got to warn Emily — no I can't get her involved yet —
God I've got to warn somebody: find out who is that *villain*. . .
Lobster-pots, he said lobster-pots. . . !

She goes.

Scene Nine

The Ralahine Co-operative. Enter CRAIG, PEASANTS, ROISIN
and MICHEAL — *they are all very respectably dressed in new
white festive smocks, and they carry garlands which they put
up round the stage. A large banner reads 'Our First Harvest:
Each for All'.* CRAIG *fussily supervises the decorating-process.*

MICHEAL (*to the audience*):
   Ah the great celebration. . . sure wouldn't you know
   When you see us all dressed like eedjits as white as the snow
   That the Englishman Craig has at last put his mark
   On the Irish barbarians brutal and dark?
   He has brought over for this harvest a marvellous machine:
   If it works, or does not work, is yet to be seen.
   Nonetheless, what he has done,
   We ourselves can make our own.
   And with this in my mind I have composed a small poem.

   'Not Vulcan nor Daedalus
   Of the ould Grecian genius
   Had ever contrived
   Such an engine so various:
   Not crafty King Solomon
   Nor proud Archimedes
   Could have dreamed in their sleep
   Of such a phenomenon — '

1ST PEASANT (*improvising*).
  'With the spin of two wheels
  We will cut in three days
  All the corn we were scything
  At each others' heels
  If the weather held good —

3RD PEASANT (*improvising*).
  For a week or a month:
  In the blaze of the heat
  Like an axe on our head — '

  — Improvise how we like in the spirit of the co-operative, it takes a true poet to think up for us Archimedes and the pagan nymphs —

1ST PEASANT. There will *be* pagan nymphs in it, with their long legs and their snow-white bosoms — ?

ROISIN. Oh there will, there will surely — Did ye ever know my brother to ever leave any of that out?

General laughter. CRAIG *leads them all out. As they go, enter* ROXANA *at one side, to attract* ROISIN'*s attention. She is still wearing her male clothes, but without a hat and her hair is long and free.*

ROXANA. Ssst — Roisin — !

ROISIN *avoids the others as they all go out.*

ROISIN. Miss Roxana — ! But you're dressed like a — but we thought you were in England — but we —

ROXANA. Ssh, don't let them see me — Roisin there are the most terrible things going on inside Ralahine. I just don't dare tell the Vandaleurs, because we've got to find out who is implicated and who knows about it, if it gets out too soon it could just *ruin* the co-operative, it would break Mr Vandaleur's heart and his poor wife — Roisin who is the man who's in charge of the lobster-fishery?

ROISIN. The lobsters, why sure it's —

ROXANA. What I have found out about that man I could send him to the *gallows* —

ROISIN. Oh my God —

ROXANA. He is using his lobsterpots as a criminal concealment for aid and comfort to the slave-trade —

Enter MICHEAL *briskly, lilting a jig and clapping his hands.*

MICHEAL. Aha, Roisin, are ye there, girl, they have the new reaping yoke dismantled from its travelling-car, and Neddy Craig is assembling it this minute in the great paddock, come on, girl, the new machine — !

ROXANA *stares at* MICHEAL *transfixed:* ROISIN *gives a moan of fear:* MICHEAL *stares at* ROXANA *first in astonishment and then in admiration. He sweeps off his hat.* (*Declaims:*)

'Oh tell me in time if you are not divine
Or a god or a goddess the senses to confuse:
Sure would glorious Diana wear the Armour of Lysander
Not a hero on earth would such a maiden refuse. . . !'

ROXANA *glares at him in horror. Bewildered by her hostility, he turns to go.*

ROISIN. Micheal!

MICHEAL *halts, and stares at the two women.*

You said lobster-pots and that's the truth. The truth also he is my brother. About the slave-trade I have heard nothing. But if you know what you know, you will tell the magistrate and have him taken?

ROXANA. Oh my God, child, your own brother. . .

ROISIN. You will have him taken, you have the proof? There are those would kill you if they knew that, and I would not be the last of them, me! Because it can not be true, not the slave-trade — no not true. Or if it is true itself, then *he* does not know what it is he is after doing.

MICHEAL (*to* ROXANA): Where did you hear this?

ROXANA. Fortescue Grange.

ROISIN. Fortescue Grange, Micheal, the very house of the marauding Orangemen!

ROISIN *goes out.*

ROXANA. May I say —

MICHEAL. May I say, before you speak, that I have indeed been
a party to the enslavement of the Ethiopian blackamoors —
and I had reasons.

ROXANA. Oh the devil of a high price in it — I know all about
that one.

MICHEAL. The height of the price, ma'am, alone, was to my mind
coherent reason. This co-operative might well fail: and if it
does, the Ralahine tenants will once again be in search of money
for whatever defence and protection they can get.

ROXANA. Yes, but the protection, the defence of the black
slaves —

MICHEAL. Ah. I take your meaning. Is it possible, do you ask me —
and do you not think I have asked myself? — to raise up the
oppressed people by the oppression of somebody else, children
of Ham and accurséd though they may be. . . ?

ROXANA. Accurséd — ! Who told you that?

MICHEAL. I was one time on my way to becoming a priest at the
seminary. It got no further because Daniel Hastings had my
father evicted: so the fees for my schooling could not be
assembled. But some instruction I did have. If, in your
opinion, it was not complete — and I see now indeed it was not
complete — I would be grateful for you to put that right.
Indeed, ma'am, for you and for the hold you have over my
spirit, I would do anything till my last day: you are an
American republican, of such kind I have never met in my
life. From an Irish republican, true service, as it were a
marriage between our two ideals. (*He takes her hand with a
gallant bow, kisses it, and turns to go.*) Believe it, within *my*
devising, there will be no more of this dirty slave-trade.

ROXANA. No — wait — please. Maybe there should be.

He pauses, surprised.

We need to do more than find out about the slave-trade. We
need to stop it, to destroy it, if we can, from *within*.

MICHEAL (*after a moment's thought*). I take your meaning.
I will continue. I will inform you. For you, everything.

Sounds of people offstage. ROXANA *runs out hurriedly.*
Enter VANDALEUR, EMILY, CRAIG *and* PEASANTS. *Two*
of the latter bring in an easel with a fancy cloth veiling a
picture.

VANDALEUR. My good friends, the golden grain is ripe for the
reaping-hook, and the reaping-hook, my good friends, being a
mechanical invention, the first time ever in this country, is the
crown on the brow of the Palladium of our success —

CRAIG. Don't we want to take a look at the official portrait of
the mechanical marvel? Mrs Vandaleur?

EMILY. Mr Craig, members of the commune — with pleasure — !

She unveils a brightly coloured representation of the reaping-
machine. Applause and a burst of music.

CRAIG. Mr Deputy Secretary, will you read the address?

1ST PEASANT (*reads*): 'To the agricultural labourers of County
Clare: this machine of ours is one of the first machines ever
given to the working classes to lighten their labour and at the
same time increase their comforts. Any kind of machinery
used for shortening labour — except used in a co-operative
society like ours — must tend to lessen wages, and to deprive
working men of employment: but, if the working-classes
would cordially and peacefully adopt our system, no power or
party could prevent their success. There would thus, under the
socialist and co-operative arrangement, be no more starvation
in the midst of abundance.' May I say, Mr Vandaleur, sir,
this address, sir, should be posted on every church-gate in the
Province of Munster.'

Applause.

VANDALEUR. And sent furthermore to every landlord throughout Ireland. I have already taken steps. For tonight, my friends,
you will all enjoy yourselves, and tomorrow let the reaping
commence. But one thing before we all give ourselves up to
the revels — to our sober, indeed biblical, revels, affording
without indulgence praise to the Lord for our communal

energy as did Boaz the Patriarch in the Book of Ruth — one thing — our intended crop of scientifically-derived winter-wheat, if sown in the great paddock as soon as the present harvest is saved, will infallibly pay for the cost of the reaping-machine: and the present harvest, if sold in the earliest market by reason of the rapidity of the reaping-machine, will infallibly pay for the capital expended already in the first stages of our most hopeful development. Congratulations to every one of you — music — Mr Secretary, will you lead Mrs Vandaleur into the first figure of the English country dance you have been at such pains to teach the people?

CRAIG. I have always maintained that the English mode of dancing has a most admirable influence towards order, method, discipline, and courtesy. We will see with what diligence my pupils have profited therefrom. . .

He forms them up to perform a polite and solemn English dance. As they dance, to one side of the stage —

Scene Nine (A)

Thompson's Tower in County Cork.
This scene takes place on the opposite side while the dance continues. THOMPSON *and* ANNA WHEELER *enter, writing letters.*

ANNA. Ma chère amie. . . Tell our fellow-socialists in France that Ralahine has truly proved the value of the co-operative system as a means toward the emancipation of women!

THOMPSON. Dear Friend. . . Once again a list of complaints from Ireland to England. No mention in Owen's *Co-operative Magazine* of my new book *Practical Directions for the Establishment of Communities.* And also no help from the English branch of the movement for my own co-operative project here in Glandore.

ANNA. The change amongst the women and children of Ralahine! The new residential school — fresh milk, green vegetables — the mothers left as free as the men all working together in the fields and dairy. . . Alas the women do not yet receive equal pay, but their votes are equal to those of the men! Mrs Craig, who runs the school, has been most tactful in regard to her Protestant persuasion — thereby happily evading the scorn of my dear Thompson who sees the dead hand of the religious Brahmins in every aspect of Irish life.

THOMPSON. God in heaven, the co-operative movement should be blazing bonfires of pure joy at the success of Craig and Vandaleur — the very first complete commune totally integrated with the indigenous people to be commenced anywhere, I believe, in the whole world — and without external finance, without any need for the *kow-tow* to our Hottentot Hibernian gentry!

ANNA. The Owenite block in the movement so frustrates all the work of my Thompson — and this, with his worsening health, casts a shadow over my life. Nonetheless his physical energies continue always to astonish me. *Entre deux amies,* in the learned language, *coitus philosophicus interruptus non est.* . . Your devoted Anna.

THOMPSON. I knew it, I knew it, *vae victis,* Daniel O'Connell has sold out the Irish multitude — in return for Catholic seats in the Westminster Babel-brothel, he has agreed to the disfranchisement of the forty-shilling freeholders — the main body of his support! My dear friend, a political vacuum, but where is the co-operative movement? If only I could live for ever — in the love of my Anna — as it is, I must make the best of a short life. I remain, Thompson.

The PEASANTS, *impatient with the decorum of the country-dance, break into an enthusiastic Irish reel —* CRAIG *and the* VANDALEURS *are willy-nilly involved in it.*

They all go out.

ACT TWO

Act Two

Scene One

Fortescue Grange. Enter BAKER-FORTESCUE *and* GENTLEMEN, *dressed for hunting, but with pistols. Hunting-calls on a horn.*

BAKER-FORTESCUE. Gentlemen! I have had this letter from the High Sheriff of County Clare! Our operations on behalf of the security forces are to cease forthwith. (*He holds out a letter which the* GENTLEMEN *angrily grab at.*) We are an offence to the leaking urine of the bloody liberal conscience. . .

1ST GENTLEMAN. The craven spirit of John Vandaleur has infected every gentleman in the county! Why cannot the Duke of Cumberland awake to the situation — he will never seize power if he delays any longer —

BAKER-FORTESCUE. It progresses — leave it alone. But today, I regret to tell you, we must content ourselves with hunting *foxes.*

The GENTLEMEN *groan, and put their pistols away.*

I thought best we should hunt Vandaleur's. That model farm of his *deserves* security from all manner of red-tailed predator.

2ND GENTLEMAN. From what I hear it has it already. Did you not know that his foxes were *shot*?

BAKER-FORTESCUE. So for Ralahine, no foxes. . . So, for Ralahine, we should follow a drag. Kitty! Have you not got that aniseed on your fetlocks yet — come here, girl! Gentlemen, you remember the traditional Fortescue drag-hunt. . . ?

Enter KITTY, *stripped to her shift, trembling. She gives a frightened curtsey.*

First one to catch her has her all to himself for the whole night!

So run for us, girl, twice as fast as the swoop of a hawk,
South for two miles, into Ralahine by the turn of the cross,
Through the home farm, and straight over the paddock —
Keep your hard young feet firm on the mire on the moss
On the stone on the rock on the corn and so after —
By God there's one bloody Teague will give thanks for the
    speed of his daughter. . . !

*He sets her off running with a crack of his whip — she speeds
off and out of sight.*

No-one's to catch her till she gets across Vandaleur's crop! Call
up the hounds, boys, whip, huntsman — we go — !

Whoops, cheers, horn, and they gallop off after her.

Scene Two

*The Ralahine Co-operative. Action continued from the previous
scene.* KITTY *re-enters, and runs about the hall, dodging and
doubling — the cries of the hunt are heard, off. A great cry of
'view hallo' as she runs clear through the middle: then she
disappears from sight by some rapid movements.* BAKER-
FORTESCUE *enters in the back of the audience amid a chorus
of baffled hunt noises, hounds yelping, desultory yells of the men
from different corners etc.*

BAKER-FORTESCUE. Gone to ground. . . ? Aha, not her! The
    paddock — we can't jump because bloody Vandaleur's staked
    his hedges!

GENTLEMEN (*off*). Oliver, Oliver — go round by the farm-yard
    — they have the gate open through to the paddock that way — !

More yells and blowings of the horn etc. Enter, on stage,
MICHEAL *and* PEASANTS.

MICHEAL. He has his hounds streaming over the great paddock
    and the winter-wheat — look sharp, boys, look sharp — or the
    horses'll be into the yard!

PEASANTS. All the work will be destroyed — for the clearing of the debt for the machinery — shut the gate, boys, shut the gate — !

With angry exclamations the PEASANTS *all join in a fierce dancing movement, to form a barrier across the stage, which* BAKER-FORTESCUE *confronts.*

BAKER-FORTESCUE. Open the gate. . . open the gate when you're told. . . God damn you, I'll cut off your — blow off your — Vandaleur — ! *Open the gate!*

PEASANTS. We will not.

Enter VANDALEUR *at a run, behind the* PEASANTS.

BAKER-FORTESCUE. Will you order your servants, John Vandaleur, to throw open this gate at once —

VANDALEUR. Major, they are not my servants, they are the members of the committee of the Ralahine Association. I am not in a position to —

BAKER-FORTESCUE *roars and points his pistol.*

If you threaten us with that weapon, sir, you will be liable to a most serious charge. Surely, your pursuit of the vulpine species does not entitle you —

BAKER-FORTESCUE *puts his pistol away.*
ROISIN *enters through the auditorium, with a basket of turf.*
BAKER-FORTESCUE *sees her and turns on her.*

BAKER-FORTESCUE. Vulpine, who the devil said *vulpine*? Every fox on this land has been shot and you know it; two legs and not four, you egregious eedjit, the greasy vixen we're after today! And begod if we've lost one there's always another —

He chases ROISIN *and tumbles her over. A yell from offstage:*

GENTLEMAN (*off*). View hallo view hallo — Oliver, look to the west, Kitty Mulroney is over the hill west — Oliver — after her — !

BAKER-FORTESCUE. View hallo — !

BAKER-FORTESCUE *goes off screaming. Hunt noises in crescendo, then they fade away. The* PEASANTS *relax their barricade delighted.*

VANDALEUR. I would have thought it would have been better to have opened, the normal courtesy of a country gentleman to his neighbours, what could I do, he called you my servants — Mr Craig! — did he say *shot*? There has been shooting of foxes on this land? Mr Craig, Mr Craig —

Enter CRAIG *at a run.*

Who gave the orders, sir, for the shooting of foxes! Utilitarian damned ignorance, is this what they call the Manchester school of economy — breaking all bonds of courtesy, comradeship through the whole district — ?

CRAIG. Excuse me, a serious problem, elimination of vermin, scientifically-co-ordinated agronomic procedures concomitant with the mechanization of — Mr Vandaleur, the continued complaints of the workpeople, as expressed within committee, outrageous depredations among the poultry, we could not tolerate —

ROISIN (*coming up on stage*). Death alive, did you not see who it was they were chasing! Did ye not see Kitty Mulroney out of Fortescue's kitchen, the creature, running her heart out up hill down dale to keep the teeth of the dogs from her back!

MICHEAL (*amid expressions of approval from the* PEASANTS). Did ye not see they would have chased my sister the same way for the same purpose, and begod she's not even one of Fortescue's own tenants!

ROISIN. Ye do not believe, surely, Mr Vandaleur, Mr Craig, 'twas the heat of the sport only brought these gentlemen into Ralahine today! Oh ho no sir, he knew well, did your purple Major, that the ploughing and sowing the great paddock was such dignity and pride to the small people of Ralahine, he had rather he'd run mad than endure it, so he would.

The PEASANTS *all acclaim this.*

MICHEAL. Mr Vandaleur, may we therefore be clear about one thing: this co-operative is organized, and well organized, by every one of its members together — and we are not the Lords and Gentlemen — we neither know, sir, nor care for the normal forms of the big-house courtesy. We do not want the fox-hunt, we have said so, and we have shown it.

ROISIN. We would be obliged for you to recognize such is now the position.

> VANDALEUR *stands awkwardly as* CRAIG *goes out with* ROISIN *and the* PEASANTS. MICHEAL *ignores him, and he goes out alone.* MICHEAL *remains behind and addresses the audience:*

MICHEAL.
At last we are proud in the proof of our power.
Let us see is it not time to do something more?
Roxana is my heart's love: and tonight she and I
Will leave the Orangeman and his damned slave-ship
Totally stranded high and dry.
Secret work: dangerous: why wouldn't we dare?
Begod I have done worse things in the name of Lady Clare.

> *He remains on stage as the scene changes.*

Scene Three

The Irish Coast. Enter ROXANA (*in female clothes*), *meeting* MICHEAL. *They embrace fervently.*

ROXANA. My darling, is there enough evidence still left at that monastery to clinch the case against Baker-Fortescue?

MICHEAL. There is. We've got him!

> *As they embrace again, they hear voices off.* MICHEAL *hastily slips out. Enter* EMILY *and* BAKER-FORTESCUE, *on opposite sides.* EMILY *embraces* ROXANA, *and stands beside her.* VANDALEUR, *agitated, hurries in and joins them. The* SERJEANT *enters with a portfolio of papers.*

SERJEANT. Be upstanding for the High Sheriff of County Clare!

> *Enter the* HIGH SHERIFF. *He takes a document from the* SERJEANT *and looks round at the company.*

HIGH SHERIFF. The lady from America, please. Madam, you pronounce yourself, here, the protagonist of an alleged adventure, last night, under cover of darkness, whereby a vessel — the — the —

ROXANA. The brig 'Maria Edgeworth'.

HIGH SHERIFF. Be silent, I have the name. You claim that this brig by complicity of an unidentified associate was induced to run aground upon the sandbank, as alleged, over *there*, thus defeating an attempt to have her loaded with illegal cargo in the furtherance of the abominable slave-trade. Serjeant! Do you see any ship on the sandbank?

SERJEANT. No sir.

ROXANA. She floated off at the ebb tide, the only place he dare take her was down-river and she's gone — it is in my affidavit!

HIGH SHERIFF. Not reported by the coastguard. Now, the cargo — where is it?

ROXANA. They had it hid in the ruined monastery. It was still there this morning at sun-up.

SERJEANT. Pursuant to your orders, sir, I checked the ruin of the monastery, the graveyard, the purlieus. No evidence of illegal storage.

ROXANA. Don't you see they will have moved them — they've had all morning to get rid of them — did you not look for hoof-prints, tracks of wheels — ?

SERJEANT. Adjacent surface of an unyielding nature, rocks and stones, dry, afforded no trace of surreptitious transport.

HIGH SHERIFF. Mr Vandaleur, *your* land, your monastery — any knowledge of such usage for the ruins?

VANDALEUR. Certainly not — but if Miss Roxana is so positive, then —

EMILY. Of course she's positive! Why I was with her myself when we heard Major Baker-Fortescue and his American agent, they were plotting, in secret —

BAKER-FORTESCUE. Oh indeed, madam, where?

EMILY. In Dublin, in the — I — I had rather not say where.

HIGH SHERIFF. This is nothing but hearsay. Most dubious hearsay. This person you allege acted as pilot to the 'Maria Edgeworth' caused her to strike upon the sandbank — where is he?

ROXANA. I gave him my word he would not be implicated.

HIGH SHERIFF. But of course he would be implicated if your story is true. An accomplice in a felony. Were he to turn King's Evidence, however —

BAKER-FORTESCUE. Draw your attention, High Sheriff, to the peril inherent in any offer of clemency to disaffected individuals of a certain religion, to incriminate a landlord, Protestant landlord, draw your attention to the unsolved murder of Daniel Hastings on this very property.

HIGH SHERIFF. Yes. . . You either produce him unconditionally, or not. But if not. . .

ROXANA. I gave my word —

The HIGH SHERIFF *ostentatiously tears up her deposition.*

BAKER-FORTESCUE. On the other hand, my *own* associate, I can and will produce, Mr Wilberforce!

Enter WILBERFORCE.

High Sheriff, Judge Ephraim Wilberforce, prominent American jurist, and my partner in my perfectly legal West Indian traffic, sugar, exotic fruits. And here are the papers to prove it.

WILBERFORCE. Well aware, sir, I have no mandate to practise the law within your jurisdiction, sir, but if this was Atlanta Georgia, and you-all had been duly sworn in the presence of *my* bench, I would proceed by — (*He registers the identity of* ROXANA *and suddenly becomes decisive instead of tentative.*) I would proceed by examination of the known character and antecedents of the principal complainant. *He* said Philadelphia — didn't I tell *her* Boston? Oho, *she* is well-known. Being the born bastard daughter of a high-yaller whore from her own father's slave-cabins!

BAKER-FORTESCUE (*choking with shock*). You mean — *she* — Jedediah — in *my* house — Jedediah Van Leyden Junior — (*He prevents himself with an effort from striking* ROXANA.) All forms of your god-damned treachery — every way, all of it, flesh, blood, spirit — be certain, *boy,* I won't forget. . . !

WILBERFORCE. She's an example, High Sheriff — you wouldn't maybe know the term — in Georgia we call it *philo-phallic race-envy* — I'd best not go into it on account of the lady's presence, but . . . (*He whispers in the* HIGH SHERIFF's *ear:*) . . . inflamed sexuality, glandular, some of 'em do it with hogs, on account, you understand, of their African heritage. . . and she has set herself these last few years to lay out false accusations and indecent scandal broadcast against no end of honourable white-folks all up and down the Atlantic seaboard!

EMILY. Roxana, your father — his wife was my own father's sister — she was —

ROXANA. His wife was not my mother. I'm sorry, what he says is quite true. At least, about that. Not the rest of it. Oh God, not the rest of it. Does it make any difference?

EMILY (*with an effort*). Difference. . . no of course not. . .

BAKER-FORTESCUE. Remarkable fine brooch, Vandaleur, like a soup-plate. . . your wife's taste. . . French?

HIGH SHERIFF (*scribbling hastily on a paper*). Under the provisions of the Peace Preservation Act, military emergency coercive draconian powers, am entitled by my office to present you, madam — (*Gives the paper to* ROXANA.) with this order for your immediate deportation from the Kingdom of Ireland. Serjeant, ensure the lady leaves for Limerick before sunset, put her personally aboard the first vessel sailing out of the port.

VANDALEUR. Upon what grounds, sir, my wife's relative — ?

HIGH SHERIFF. I have defined her as an undesirable. And she is *not* your wife's relative. . . Oliver, the black stallion, you know we discussed a price, now I have had another offer from Colonel O'Brien. . .

He and BAKER-FORTESCUE *withdraw, talking horses.* WILBERFORCE *tags along with them.*

ROXANA. Don't you realise they had the whole thing arranged before they got here — Emily, you must help me — that cargo can be no more than five miles away — make immediate inquiries, surely someone in the co-operative —

VANDALEUR. The co-operative. Don't *you* realise, the reputation of my co-operative has all but been destroyed before my face with your meddling and muddling!

EMILY. Don't you realise that the High Sheriff was trying to *save* the co-operative, Roxana! Don't you realise the Rapist Fortescue would do everything he could to put the blame for that cargo upon Mr Vandaleur, had it been found in the ruins — and my God what a relief that they had managed to get rid of it!

ROXANA. Do you mean to tell me that you all know that my story was quite true! And yet you allowed them to serve me with — (*She flourishes the deportation order.*)

EMILY. Roxana, my dear Roxana — it is not as though you were really my cousin any longer, but — Of course we all knew it was true. Mr Vandaleur indeed confronted that horrible Fortescue, with his guilt. Made him swear never again would he so much as *breathe* toward a slave-agent!

VANDALEUR. Or else, no stone unturned before absolute exposure! And moreover he must refrain from harassment of our co-operative —

EMILY. Roxana, do you hear, Mr Vandaleur made him swear, upon his honour as a gentleman.

VANDALEUR. I have lived in this country all my life, as a gentleman. Philosophically scientifically endeavoured to lift up the poor people toward a condition of humanity. Out of what? Out of slavery. *My* slaves, and I am responsible. My co-operative the sole token of the responsibility of my life, my status in society, I live *here.* It's a question of blood.

VANDALEUR *goes.*

ROXANA.
Such blood indeed as we all now comprehend

In my light body to be of such a kind
Stained in my very womb by the womb's blood of my mother —

EMILY. Roxana, my darling, no stain in your spirit, your mind —

ROXANA.
Nonetheless, where I am one
And in this island all alone
You know yourselves to be the other.
There is no doubt your co-operative must be saved from its
ruin:
For if it fail, the black slaves, who are not saved, will reap
no gain. . .

ROXANA *goes with the* SERJEANT.

EMILY (*to the audience*).
I am made small by her fortitude
By the width of the wound
That this news has laid open in her side:
In my own heart.
From now there is but part
Of me beneath my husband in his bed
To furnish love
Toward him as a good wife should.
The rest must rove
With my heart's darling wherever she goes
Far over far over the gray Atlantic wave. . .

EMILY *goes.*

Re-enter BAKER-FORTESCUE *and* WILBERFORCE.

WILBERFORCE. Reckon you didn't appreciate, Major, old Judge
Ephraim and his intelligence service could operate so far and
so fast. . . ?

BAKER-FORTESCUE. Far enough. Shall we try for a change a
little bit nearer home? This turd of a Teague fisherman
brought my ship upon the sandbank — where's he gone? Find
him out — and find out how we can hang him! Anything,
anything, to incriminate the rabble of Ralahine!

They go.

Scene Four

Thompson's Tower in County Cork. Enter THOMPSON, *very ill, staggering about with his arms full of papers. Noise, off, people shouting, and* ANNA's *voice expostulating.*

THOMPSON. Keep them out, my rapacious relatives, I will not have them at my death-bed, Anna, keep them out — !

> ANNA *enters, the* LAWYER *behind her. She disposes* THOMPSON *into an arm-chair, tucks a rug around him. There is a large black-draped jar on a small table at his side marked 'For the Head of Wm. Thompson.'*

Down, dog, to your basket — who's this — it is not that damned clergyman, the pundit, the brahmin, the rabbi, the mad mullah of Trinity College — ?

ANNA. Your attorney — you asked for him, you know who he is — (*She finds a paper and gives it to the lawyer.*) Here is the will, please look through it carefully and correct it before he signs it.

THOMPSON (*snatching it*). No, no, he will endeavour to dissuade me — only way, do it all yourself, so — so — (*He reads through the paper, making sweeping corrections to it.*) *Fait accompli,* you see — so! Where's the sawbones? He should be here. Dammit, Anna, do I have to take my own pulse to the very last?

ANNA. I don't want to know about that surgeon. He can't cure you, he can only —

THOMPSON. Collect my head for the phrenologist — Monsieur Pierre Baume of Paris, to whom it has been promised — and why not? For the philosophers the authenticated brain-box of a philosopher — the complexity of life, as I always say — infinite: through his head and his books, they will deduce the complex soul of Thompson, and by God they will be wrong! Anna, I *told* you, *your* head as well, mouth-to-mouth, nose-to-nose, cuddling up in the same jar. . . !

ANNA. Romantic — but impractical.

THOMPSON. You are about to say I am a hypocrite. We shared

our bed, we shared our book-writing, page between page, we shared everything all these years —

ANNA. With men, it is a common condition.

THOMPSON. As we have abundantly proven within the argument of our joint works. Our joint works with *my* name on them. But common should be curable. I mean *this* man, Anna, *me,* all of my life — have *I* not worked hard enough to rid myself of it, Anna, of *some* of it. . . ? Anna?

ANNA. Your ideas have been presented. If they are true and you are not, does it matter?

THOMPSON. It does if they are not in truth *my* ideas. I am asking my betrayed collaborator, Anna, for God's sake to tell me the truth!

ANNA. This world of competitive enterprise demands each new idea be the jealously-guarded property of but one individual.

THOMPSON. I have called all property *theft!*

ANNA. So there you are, the new idea — and you, the landed gent, necessarily the proprietor of it. . . What else is this will but the chart of the buried treasure of an old pirate hanged in his chains?

> You will not see before you die —
> And Thompson, Thompson, neither will I —
> The fad of the rich become the faith of the poor
> And your crushed heart like an underground dungeon
> At last able to fling open its door. . .

THOMPSON. And yet what has been happening at Ralahine, Anna! Like a city set upon an hill for the world to wonder at! I craved only that Glandore, down there, through the window, do you observe the half-finished brickwork? — craved only to redeem our own New Jerusalem, our own complete co-operative, from the obscurity of paper and watch it flourishing before I died. And here, no not *there* — (*The* LAWYER *is looking at the documents* —) Not the paper — through the window — *here* there would be no landlord — not the tittle of a title of Proprietor nor *ex-officio* President throughout the whole constitution! Self-electing, democratic, beholden to no High Priest, no Owen, no John Scott Vandaleur, not even a Neddy Craig! The people alone to control, through their communal wisdom. I *must* have it all set down.

ANNA. Attorney, for God's sake help him. He must have his will completed with the constitution of the co-operative truly established in legal terms, so the trustees, to whom he leaves everything —

THOMPSON. No no not everything: there is an annuity for my dear Anna —

LAWYER. To whom, sir, you are not married, and she is not a blood-relative. . . Oh dear oh dear, this testament, I foresee vast complications. . . It will inevitably be contested by your family, you realise that?

THOMPSON. They shall not get one penny — Hottentots, Orange Mohawks, the cormorants of the Irish common-weal — !

Enter the SURGEON. RELATIVES *attempt to follow him.* ANNA *repulses them, and then turns to find the* SURGEON *taking out some medicine.*

SURGEON. Dear lady, he must not excite himself —

ANNA. Why not, it is the last thing left for him. And he don't want loblolly, he wants to talk, don't he?

THOMPSON. You came to measure it, so measure it. If you don't they will infallibly attempt an exchange when I am dead.

The SURGEON *starts to measure his head and makes notes of it.*

LAWYER. I do fear, Mr Thompson, so frequent in such cases, the whole estate to be swallowed in costs. And I have grave doubts the law will not recognise this — this fictional commune —

ANNA. Fictional! It already exists, look there out of the window —

THOMPSON. Get Flanagan, get him quick — fictional — no no no no no no no — !

As he cries out, ANNA *hurries off, shouting* 'Mr Flanagan!'

The RELATIVES *push past her and crowd in.* THOMPSON
lies back, eyes closed, exhausted.

1ST RELATIVE (*as* ANNA, *re-entering, tangles with them all*).
Where is the will?

2ND RELATIVE (*grabbing the will*). Here is the will!

3RD RELATIVE (*snatching it from the* 2ND RELATIVE).
Good Lord, it's not been signed!

ANNA. Give that to me —

1ST RELATIVE. Too late, madam, no signature — he is dead
and the will invalid!

There is a struggle over the document. FLANAGAN *enters.*

THOMPSON (*surprising them all*). Ah, Flanagan — you finished
that community-centre yet?

FLANAGAN. Have the roof on by the end of the week,
Mr Thompson.

1ST RELATIVE. His *building contractor. . . ?*

2ND and 3RD RELATIVES. Absolutely, he is out of his mind.

THOMPSON. Tonight, not next week, I should have lived to see
the roof — nonetheless, it is *not* fictional! Flanagan, you're a
witness — Sawbones, so are you! I put my name upon this
document.

He signs the will. FLANAGAN *and the* SURGEON *do so too,
as witnesses. The* PARSON *enters with a bible.*

God in Heaven — who is that!

PARSON. God in Heaven, Mr Thompson, indeed. I am informed
you are about to depart, a most dread and uncharted journey.
Behold, sir, I bring you the form of your itinerary —

ANNA. Cannot you see he has not finished his packing! Out
out out —

THOMPSON (*leaping up*). Out out out — !

They drive the PARSON *and the* RELATIVES *out. The*
LAWYER *and* SURGEON *follow.* THOMPSON *shakes hands
with* FLANAGAN *as the latter goes out.*

Yes, a journey — oh Anna, my dearest love, flesh of my flesh,
bone of my bone, dream of my deepest dream — why can you
not come with me. . . ?

They go out.

Scene Five

The Ralahine Co-operative. Enter CRAIG.

CRAIG. Fellow-members of the Ralahine Co-operative
Association: before we resume our wonted labours this
morning, I would ask you all to stand for a few moments to
pay tribute to the memory of Mr William Thompson. We must
never forget that our great co-operative movement owes almost
as much to the men of intellect as it does to those who pursue
its purposes, as it were, spade in hand. Be that as it may, by
his death we are all bereft.

A short solemn silence. CRAIG *puts on his hat and leaves the
stage — as he goes, he meets* EMILY, *and takes off his hat,
briefly and mournfully, to greet her.*

Enter ROXANA, *wearing a lady's travelling costume, quite
different from her previous outfit.* EMILY *runs towards her
with a joyous cry, but* ROXANA *puts her finger to her lips
with an urgent gesture.*

EMILY. Roxana — oh my love — but of course — you are
forbidden! You have broken the law to come back here — ?
But my darling, how? Where did you go, what did you do, for
what reason do you —

ROXANA (*cutting the torrent short*). Not a word to Mr Vandaleur —

EMILY. My dear heart, oh my sweet, I wouldn't dream, no not
one word —

ROXANA (*cutting it short again*). They put me out, I went to
England, I went to America, to Jamaica — I came back.
And I have found out at last how to prove everything about
Baker-Fortescue. But not here — I must go to Dublin. There

will be documents in the port of Dublin in possession of the
master of the 'Maria Edgeworth', next month. She is due
to dock there on a voyage between —

EMILY. But why do you come here?

ROXANA. In case anything goes wrong, someone in Ireland must
know what I am doing.

Enter ROISIN *in a flurry, as the* HIGH SHERIFF, BAKER-
FORTESCUE, VANDALEUR *and* HAGAN *enter noisily
behind.*

ROISIN. There's the High Sheriff and the red soldiers, they're
all over the home farm — they said something about Micheal —
they have a warrant for arrest!*

ROXANA. My God, they're coming after him for what he did
to the 'Maria Edgeworth'! My God, if that's true, they'll be —

EMILY. They'll be coming after *you!* Go with Roisin, get hold
of Micheal, go down by the path through the woods — oh
hurry hurry hurry — oh my love — !

She and ROXANA *exchange an embrace —* ROXANA *and*
ROISIN *then flee.*

HIGH SHERIFF (*this dialogue to start at * above*). A question
of harbouring fugitives, I am sorry, Vandaleur, the information
is specific, we have the man's name and evidence against him
on a sworn affidavit. I have had no choice but draw up a
warrant.

VANDALEUR. I have absolutely no idea what it is you are
talking about. Man, name, fugitive — ? Who? And why is the
Major here — and who is this?

SERGEANT (*offstage*). You that way, you that way, round the
back there one man — move! You, through the front garden,
two potting-sheds and a summer-house, make sure that they're
clear!

EMILY. Mr Vandaleur, pray, invite the gentlemen up to the
house.

HIGH SHERIFF. Most unfortunate shadow upon the good work

of your co-operative — fear prevalent for some time such idealistic institutions leave the way far too wide for subversive manipulation. The man we want is Michael Sullivan, known to his friends as Slippery Mick.

VANDALEUR. Micheál O Súilleabháin, supervisor of our lobster-fisheries. A most responsible man. Slippery Mick? Nonsense — never heard of it. We do not permit nicknames.

HIGH SHERIFF. But you *do* permit murder? If you are hiding him here I must close down your co-operative.

VANDALEUR. This is surely not possible — he is —

BAKER-FORTESCUE. I will tell you what he is — the denounced killer of your man Daniel Hastings, so what d'you think of that? And you promote him to *supervise*! Hagan, say your piece.

HAGAN. Mr Vandaleur, you know me. In the days I was permitted to sell a small measure of porter to the rural people and they thirsty from the hard work, Slippery Mick and his brave boys was constant customers at my bar. Upon the night of Hastings' death, sir, they rose up and went out with the womens' shawls about them, so. And this is the shawl that he wore. I take oath to it.

BAKER-FORTESCUE. It was found the following morning beside Hastings' dead body.

Upon a sign from BAKER-FORTESCUE, HAGAN *goes.*

VANDALEUR. Daniel Hastings died by *my* default, and therefore I regard myself as the only murderer in this community. Arrest me! I intend to hunt down no other man for it.

The noise of SOLDIERS *shouting to each other, offstage. A pause. The* SERJEANT *enters.*

SERGEANT. Seems like the bugger's gone, sir, not a trace of him.

HIGH SHERIFF (*to* VANDALEUR): When we find him it is probable that proceedings will lie against you.

The HIGH SHERIFF *and the* SERJEANT *go.*

BAKER-FORTESCUE. Probable. . . ? If *he* shirks his duty be very certain *I* won't stand idle. I said from the start this dogs-

vomit co-operative was a stalking-horse for revolution — proved,
Vandaleur, proved — Lady Clare and her Brave Boys, hey — and
you knew that I knew this and because you knew I knew it,
you dredged up that abortion of a yarn about the slave-trade,
hey? Tried to fix the Rapist Fortescue before he could fix you?

EMILY. Major Fortescue, it was not Mr Vandaleur who —

BAKER-FORTESCUE (*acknowledging her presence for the first
time*). Oh indeed, we're in mixed company. . . Have you a
notion just *how* mixed? Did you notice, the last occasion,
abortive slave-trade day, did you notice then how your
gracious lady refused to say where she met the excellent
Wilberforce? Did you ask her afterwards to amplify? Bet you
didn't, you didn't dare. Put the question to her now, go on,
man, go on, where was she when she —

VANDALEUR. Do you attempt, sir, to compromise Mrs
Vandaleur in my presence! Implication that she conceals from
her husband certain —

EMILY. Mr Vandaleur, I do not conceal. You never pressed me,
I did not say — but I will. Roxana and myself went unescorted
to the Hell Fire Club, the night you left Dublin for Manches —

VANDALEUR. No you could not have done that — they do not
permit ladies within that club, I know perfectly well.

BAKER-FORTESCUE. These ladies were dressed as men.

VANDALEUR. You suggest that my wife's purposes in — in a
place where she could not have been — were salacious?

BAKER-FORTESCUE. They kissed and cuddled in a room full
of bucks like Mother and Father Baboon in a public zoo.

VANDALEUR *strikes him.*

Ha. My honour, as an officer and gentleman — I demand
satisfaction.

EMILY. My honour as the wife of a gentleman has been
compromised by these accusations. I demand the opportunity
to explain the whole story —

VANDALEUR. Have the goodness to keep out of this! Your
ignorant interruptions are reflecting upon my honour.

BAKER-FORTESCUE. Time and place? My friends will wait upon yours.

VANDALEUR. No they won't, we'll do it now.

BAKER-FORTESCUE. Without seconds?

VANDALEUR. Why not? Are you afraid, sir, to stand on your own? Emily, my pistols!

EMILY. You haven't got any pistols, and if you had, you wouldn't know how to use them — Mr Vandaleur, will you come to your senses!

BAKER-FORTESCUE. You have no pistols? As it happens, I have two. Both loaded, you take one.

(*He pulls a pair of pistols from his belt.*) Choose.

VANDALEUR *takes one of them. They turn back to back.*

VANDALEUR. Emily, you drop your handkerchief.

EMILY *is holding her handkerchief, helplessly.*

When she drops it, ten paces, turn and fire.

A pause while EMILY *dithers. Several* PEASANTS *come in all around.*

PEASANTS. Come on, boys, my God, the gentry are having a faction-fight — every man to support Vandaleur — *etcetera. . .*

EMILY *bursts into tears.*

VANDALEUR. Take that handkerchief from your eyes, woman, will you hold it out and *drop it!*

EMILY (*suddenly stops weeping*). John Vandaleur, I am ashamed. This is totally ridiculous. What I did in the Hell Fire Club from now on shall be *my* business. I shall tell neither you nor anyone else anything about it whatever. The wife of the President of the Ralahine Commune should be above suspicion. If she is not, then I am bound to question the very basis of this co-operative! — freedom of thought, mutual harmony, democratic discussion, enlightened intercourse between the sexes. John Vandaleur, I say fiddle-dee-dee, you are a hypocrite — and a bloody fool.

She stalks out, unconsciously dropping the handkerchief as she goes. BAKER-FORTESCUE *and* VANDALEUR *have been staring at the handkerchief like automata all through her speech, they immediately start to walk, counting 'one two three —' up to 'ten'. At 'ten' they both turn and level their weapons.*

A PEASANT (*near* BAKER-FORTESCUE, *and very loud*). Hooray for the Major!

FORTESCUE *fires, but has been startled by the shout. He misses.*

BAKER-FORTESCUE. Dammit you raving eedjit, you caused me to miss! (VANDALEUR'*s pistol misses fire.*) Misfire!

VANDALEUR (*fumbling with the trigger*). Something wrong here with the flintlock —

VANDALEUR'*s pistol goes off, terrifying him. The bullet hits* BAKER-FORTESCUE *across the midriff — his belt-buckle flies off and his trousers fall down. The* PEASANTS *cheer exuberantly.*

Good God, I never intended —

PEASANTS (*rushing at him and lifting him shoulder-high*). Sean Vandaleur for King, the best shot in the whole of the west, Sean Vandaleur the only man to fly the breeches-belt beyond the skyline — *etc.*

BAKER-FORTESCUE.
  Some filthy Frenchman taught you that,
  You planned and tricked your way to it all through —
  One day, my friend, and not too long
  I too will have my laughing game with you.

BAKER-FORTESCUE *goes out furiously, amidst the jeers and mockery of the* PEASANTS, *who then carry* VANDALEUR *out the length of the audience. Before they complete their movement,* CRAIG *enters on stage, a paper in his hand. He motions to the* 1ST PEASANT, *who leaves his fellows, joins* CRAIG, *and checks the list with him.*

CRAIG. Mr Deputy-Secretary! 'Total food and lodging eighty-one persons: six pound seven and fourpence ha'penny —

averaging per week less than one shilling and sevenpence
each . . .. Four hundred forty-six quarts of new milk at one
penny per quart: one pound seventeen and two. Potatoes and
other vegetables: two pound thirteen six. Butter, twelve and a
penny; pork, nineteen sevenpence ha'penny: comes to one
eleven eight and a half. Cottage rent four and three; turf for
fuel, ninepence: five bob.'

They go, still checking the paper.

Scene Six

*The Hill of Howth overlooking Dublin Bay. Moonlight. Sounds
of a distant bell-buoy at intervals. Enter* ROISIN *and* MICHEAL,
furtively.

MICHEAL. Is this the place? It's very open, if anyone followed
us — who's that?

ROISIN. A bush of gorse in the moonlight. Stay still, keep your
face out to sea. Micheal, have you said anything yet to
Roxana about —

MICHEAL. I have not.

ROISIN. But how do you expect you are going to go with her
unless she is told —

ROXANA (*calling softly, offstage*). Roisin, oh Roisin — ?

MICHEAL. Here she comes.

ROISIN *answers with a cry like a seagull.*

Begod, if I do not tell her now, I will never be getting out of
this country at all.

ROXANA *hurries in, softly — she whistles,* ROISIN *answers,
they all come together.*

ROXANA (*breathless*). Fine, fine 'n'dandy, all in Dublin fixed
like we wanted it. I saw the lawyer whose name was given
me by the committee in Philadelphia, quite right he does have
the ear of the First Secretary at Dublin Castle. We carry on
just like I said —

MICHEAL. Madam —

> ROXANA *looks at him in surprise at the formality of his stance.*

I must inform you, you have let yourself believe what you should maybe not have believed. That I am with you on this affair only because I have loved you — and yet that is true. That I am with you only because I am concerned to give you help to prevent the slave-trade — and yet that is true too — God knows it is true. But the first reason, the chief reason: I have come all across Ireland with you in such secrecy because I need to escape, through your means, to America, but for nothing at all to do with that slave-ship.

> *A pause.* ROXANA *looks at him. He moves away, and starts again.*

'Twas a scorching hot day, we were reaping the harvest for the home-farm, we had a can of cool water, now and then the men took breath and a full swallow to keep going. Daniel Hastings came down to us, the length of the long field, his wife's good sweet tea brimming him up to the corners of his mouth. 'Too damn slow', he said. 'Refractory buggers, ye have the can there for no reason but to cost Sean Vandaleur time and money — he pays me to bloody save it for him.' And he kicked over the water, trod it into the dry stubble till every drop of it was lost. Oh a small trick, but it was the latest of all his mean-minded tricks and therefore the worst. It brought upon him his death. Because he is dead, we have now the co-operative. And the police have the papers out upon *me*. It was me that put the bullet into Daniel Hastings — it was me wrote the poem that they found on his door, madam.

ROISIN. I was the one that had taken it there and nailed it, madam.

> *A pause. Suddenly* ROXANA *sees something out at sea.*

ROXANA. There he is, that's the signal, a white light three times. The 'Maria Edgeworth' has dropped anchor outside the harbour like they said. We give them three white flashes back,

the captain puts off in his boat to the bottom of this cliff —
(*She takes a dark lantern from inside her cloak and flashes
it three times.*) When he gets to the shore he will whistle and
we go down to him. . . . Ever since we left Ralahine, you have
been calling me 'Roxana'. But just now, you said 'madam'. But
I am not. I am one of the Children of Ham, and accurséd.

A pause. MICHEAL *looks at her. She moves away and starts
again.*

Upon my twenty-first birthday, the City of Boston, a great
meeting of the Anti-Slavery Association. My father, most
popular speaker, upon the platform, a huge placard of a naked
black man, kneeling, his chains broken, his hands uplifted
to heaven and a white hand out of heaven holding the Bible
above his head. My father's voice all of a sudden in the midst
of his discourse broken with sobs — the huge audience
astonished — not me. *My* astonishment already made for me
in emotional privacy the previous evening. 'Brothers and
sisters', he shouted, 'if this our movement is not totally
open and candid before the Lord, we are as dust in the nostrils
of enlightened mankind. Therefore it is meet that I make my
confession: my fair daughter, whom you know and love, is
not — as you have been led to believe, as indeed she until last
night had been led to believe — she is not the child of my wife.
But of the slave-woman who attended to the worldly surface
of my wife, put on her clothes for her, dressed her hair. As you
know, many years ago, I gave their freedom to all my slaves.
Yet my young daughter I still held within the vile servitude of
a cowardly lie. Today I make recompense to her and to all of
you.' And they clapped and they cheered, they wept tears,
they slobbered my cheeks. That very day all those young
gentlemen from the most elegant evangelical abolitionist
Boston families who were invited to my birthday party
mysteriously fell ill of the ague or goddammit the *gout*, and
the work I continue to do for the Association, by general
agreement I have done most of it in *Europe*. I never thought of
not doing it. Because once having known freedom, till I
discovered that by inheritance in my birthplace I had no right
to it — I cannot get out of my head, out of my bowels, all the

horror of those thousands who had to make my discovery
before they were even able to walk.

*A pause. She speaks now direct to the audience, moving from
speech into a song — (Air: 'The Red-Haired Man's Wife')*:

Whereas *my* walk, my work through this world
I had made up my mind
Must be always alone, without hope, without help
From any one of my own kind —

'For how could I find any kind of myself in this world —
And yet now I allow this young man to believe that the hold
Of true love in my soul for his beauty had at last been declared,
That the truth of his touch on my body was taken and
    shared. . . ?'

MICHEAL (*sings*):
'So nearer and nearer to the land of America we rove,
The silver and gold of freedom's stronghold to be proved:
Don't I know that the truth of her touch on my body will lie
To enkindle no longer than the sting of a quick summer fly.'

ROXANA (*sings*):
'And yet I can not and I will not refuse to proclaim
These days of green leaf and white flower on the spike of
    the thorn — '

MICHEAL (*singing now to* ROXANA).
'Let the branches of winter once more rear up dark in the air
Like the arms of a slave in his chains — '

MICHEAL *and* ROXANA (*singing*):
'— yet we do not despair. . . '

They hold hands for a moment.

ROISIN (*sings — air: 'Spanish Ladies'*):
'O where will we be when the voyage has ended
O where will we be when the ship comes to port?
Sure I think there's no reason to curse our creation
We will all of us live longer than ever we have thought.'

For this Ralahine Co-operative, who was I before it was made?
Roisin Wry-neck, that's the name they had for me, runs one-
two-three, *bump* two-three, one-two-three *bump*. But oh in

the end, what glory came out of it? I am Member of Committee, Mistress Roisin in my own right — and all that I do is what they all do — and we *all* decided. . . !

MICHEAL. Roisin, I never thought of it, you did not tell them at Ralahine you were going away — when you get back to the co-operative you must explain yourself or be expelled. If you do explain, will you not be incriminated, giving aid to your brother on the run?

ROISIN. Death alive, boy, you know better than that. Within the co-operative we are all agreed, we do not bring the law, the police into our affairs. Even the Englishman, Craig, by this time understands how the people will feel about that. No no, we are all safe as regards Ralahine.

A sharp whistle, as from a bosun's pipe, offstage.

MICHEAL. My God, there's your man come ashore to us already.

WILBERFORCE *crosses the back of the stage, watching them.*

ROXANA. Do we all know what we're doing? I have here the document I brought with me from Philadelphia: he'll have the other one, the extract from the ship's papers — with the two put together and brought up before the authorities we have the evidence to cook Fortescue like a mess of clam chowder. Let's go!

They go.

Scene Seven

The Shelbourne Hotel, Dublin. Enter several GENTLEMEN, *with* BAKER-FORTESCUE. *They lounge around, smoking.* VANDALEUR *enters, with his overcoat and hat etc., and his carpet-bag, which he deposits modestly in the corner. The* GENTLEMEN *notice him.* BAKER-FORTESCUE *moves quietly out of sight behind a potted plant.*

1ST GENTLEMAN. Good heavens, it's Vandaleur! Scarcely expected to find you in Dublin, by Jove — we all believed you were single-handedly abolishing poverty in County Clare!

They all crowd round him warmly and shake his hand.

2ND GENTLEMAN. But of course he's in Dublin, Jasper, haven't you seen the posters? John Scott Vandaleur Esquire to lecture at the Rotunda upon the success of his communal agriculture — and by George, sir, though I was the first to abuse you for it in the past, your success is indeed notorious!

1ST GENTLEMAN. Notorious and deserved. Not another man in Ireland could have kept his wages down, put his total rent up, and kept all the people happy, by God! And by God everyone else in the country is following his example! It's in the newspapers. By your achievement, crimes of violence in County Clare non-existent. Ah, this military emergency —

2ND GENTLEMAN. Isn't it time, John, for government to call the whole thing off?

VANDALEUR. Ah. Yes — my exact conclusion. I have an appointment tomorrow morning with the Lord Lieutenant, gentlemen, for no other purpose. I shall use all my best endeavours. In the meantime, tonight, my lecture—

1ST GENTLEMAN. Oh be certain we shall all be there — in support of the good cause —

GENTLEMEN. Oh by Jove, yes, certainly, by George, the good cause. . . ah, yes, yes, of course —

They indulge in a nodding and nudging business between the two of them.

2ND GENTLEMAN. John, to be frank, this little meeting, not exactly by chance.

1ST GENTLEMAN. The two of us, you see — we are commissioned to — as it were, waylay you.

2ND GENTLEMAN. Oliver Baker-Fortescue. The fact is, ever since you — ah — that unhappy affair —

1ST GENTLEMAN. The breeches-belt — no need for details —

2ND GENTLEMAN. Dammit, Vandaleur, the poor fellow took his humiliation devilish hard. He wants to apologise.

1ST GENTLEMAN. I thought more than apologise. I thought he was already thinking —

2ND GENTLEMAN. Not until he knows his apology is accepted, Jasper.

1ST GENTLEMAN. John Vandaleur with a loaded pistol has proved himself no man to trifle with!

2ND GENTLEMAN. Well, sir, what d'you say? He really is most frightful ashamed.

VANDALEUR. But of course if my neighbour apologises, I accept with the greatest goodwill. Baker-Fortescue and I have known each other for years and —

1ST GENTLEMAN. Then you'll be all the more delighted that he quite seriously intends to turn Fortescue Grange into a co-operative — on the Ralahine model and he requests —

2ND GENTLEMAN. — he requests, in all earnestness, that you loan him the services of that Manchester miracle-man of yours, what's his name — ?

VANDALEUR. Mr Craig? But of course of course — why gentlemen, this is marvellous —

1ST GENTLEMAN (*having been round the potted plant*). Ah, John, I don't know how you'll take this, but poor old Oliver — behind the shrubbery — too embarrassed, silly fellow, to come out and brave the thunderstorm —

GENTLEMEN. Come on, Oliver, come on, it's quite all right, he's as happy as a sandboy!

BAKER-FORTESCUE *emerges and sheepishly shakes hands with* VANDALEUR.

BAKER-FORTESCUE. No no, don't say a word, I heard it all. John, you are a white man, dammit as white as whitewash. Look here, we must have a bumper, celebrate the buried hatchet, pipe of peace —

VANDALEUR. I do have to be at the Rotunda in a couple of hours —

BAKER-FORTESCUE. I would ask you to come with us

beforehand, except I know you have your principles —

1ST GENTLEMAN. In fact, on our way, you see, to the tempta-
tions of the Hell Fire Club —

2ND GENTLEMAN. And we know you never gamble.

BAKER-FORTESCUE. Ah dammit, must postpone the pleasure,
devilish pity — would very much liked to have had a long chat!

VANDALEUR. Now gentlemen, this is not fair, you make me
labour under obligation to you —

1ST GENTLEMAN. If he does come, he need not play: absolutely
no obligation to do *that*.

VANDALEUR. But in that case you would feel, perhaps, I was
lacking in the proper spirit —

ALL except VANDALEUR. Not at all not at all not at all
not at all. . . !

VANDALEUR. Ah, well then — perhaps — yes.

*They group themselves into a stylized posture as the scene
changes.*

Scene Eight

The Hell Fire Club. A Faro table set up by a CROUPIER. *The
game commences. The* GENTLEMEN *and* BAKER-FORTESCUE
play with a great deal of infectious laughter. VANDALEUR
watches them, intently, his excitement growing all the time.

CROUPIER. Gentlemen — sportsmen stake your wagers for the
Imperial Game of Faro. . . Captain Prendergast wins, one
hundred guineas. . . Mr Butler wins, seventy-five guineas. . .
Captain Prendergast again, fifty guineas. . . Standoff, no bets
paid. . . House wins, no bets paid. . . House wins again, no
bets paid. . . *etcetera.*

VANDALEUR *suddenly makes up his mind, and lays chips on
the table.*

Four is the loser, six is the winner — Mr Vandaleur wins — twenty-five guineas.

VANDALEUR *moves away from the table with his winnings.*

Are you leaving the game, sir?

VANDALEUR. Ah, yes, apologies, I must, my lecture at the Rotunda.

CROUPIER. It is the custom at the Hell Fire Club for gentlemen in good fortune to allow their fellow-sportsmen to regain their losses before taking leave of the table. You'll not wish to rebuff tradition, Mr Vandaleur, I'm sure. . .

VANDALEUR. I — ah — my lecture — there should be a carriage at the door. . .

He freezes in the act of putting on his coat, and addresses the audience.

I did not expect to win.
I do not want to go on.
I cannot endure to go out.
Oh God, have they got me caught?
I had not played this game
Not felt erect in me this creeping lechery of shame
This sacrificial avaricious tumult of self-exposure
So to command me nerve and brain
And quivering fragment of my frightened loin
I had not felt — since I was twenty-one
This need, this hunger, this desire today as then . . .
Again. . . ? Again. . . ?
Why gentlemen, my friends — I did not expect to win. . .

He takes off his coat and returns to the table.

I don't like these stakes — twenty-five guineas a chip not nearly sufficient, no room for them on the board — agreed, agreed, gentlemen, we raise it to fifty? The house will accommodate? Good. Play — we all play. . . !

CROUPIER. King loses, Queen wins. Major Baker-Fortescue the winner, five hundred guineas. . . Major Baker-Fortescue again, four hundred and fifty. . .

BAKER-FORTESCUE. Raise the stakes! One hundred a chip.

CROUPIER. Is that agreeable to the gentlemen? The house will accept it. . . The house wins, no bets paid. . . The house wins again, gentlemen, no bets paid. . .

VANDALEUR. Raise the stakes, raise 'em again — two hundred a chip — I insist!

CROUPIER. Discard ten, nine loses, seven wins, Major Baker-Fortescue two thousand. . . . Four cards only left in the deck, gentlemen, the house pays four-to-one if you guess their correct order — Mr Vandaleur?

VANDALEUR. Six-to-one, six-to-one — I know it, I have it — at this stage of the game only the scientific mind can correctly estimate the extent of hazard — !

CROUPIER. Four-to-one only the house odds, if you want a larger stake, make a side-bet with the Major. . . . With the stakes so very large, gentlemen, upon bets with the house we would be glad for some small class of guarantee. . .

VANDALEUR (*scribbling a bill*). Yes of course, yes, paper — I O U, J S V, good for anywhere in Ireland — Ralahine, you've heard of it, flourishing, flourishing, a co-operative estate, all of it — prosperity — !

BAKER-FORTESCUE. You're already acquainted, Colquhoun, with *my* guarantors.

CROUPIER (*getting a series of significant nods from the* GENTLEMEN). Of course, Major.

VANDALEUR. Oliver, Oliver — a side-bet — ten-to-one — do you dare, do you dare — ?

BAKER-FORTESCUE *glances round at the* GENTLEMEN.

1ST GENTLEMAN. Oliver, this is serious, you don't really intend to go on?

BAKER-FORTESCUE (*grim and implacable*). John Vandaleur from the beginning has been the victor upon every turn. I have not even begun to masticate my revenge.

(*To the audience*):
  I have so often heard them say
  That a moral man who will not play
  At cards at women at the buttock of a smooth young boy
  Knows far too well how far he would enjoy
  Such huge excess, were he just once to let his fear
  Be loosened just one button-hole. . . John Vandaleur
  Is such an one. I knew it. I have proved it — and I have
  Him now cascading maybe even to the grave.

2ND GENTLEMAN. Come on, Oliver, you're afraid of it, you're holding back your stakes!

1ST GENTLEMAN. Bear in mind, Oliver, he opposed the Act of Union.

2ND GENTLEMAN. Bear in mind, Oliver, he advocated Catholic Emancipation in Parliament.

1ST GENTLEMAN. Bear in mind he has ruined our farming with his new-fangled science, his machine-methods, his —

BAKER-FORTESCUE (*to* VANDALEUR): Done!

VANDALEUR. Eight hundred guineas — no, one thousand, Oliver — done? Five, Nine, Ten, Six!

BAKER-FORTESCUE. Five, Nine, Ten, *Five.*

VANDALEUR. No — Six — not two Fives, there is one Six left in the deck!

BAKER-FORTESCUE. Colquhoun?

CROUPIER (*turning out the last four cards*). Five, Nine, Ten —

VANDALEUR. No, wait, wait — Oliver — Fifty-to-one it's a Six not a Five!

BAKER-FORTESCUE. Done.

CROUPIER (*revealing the last card*). Five.

VANDALEUR. Another pack, another game, come on come on come on —

He grabs at the cards furiously, scatters chips all over the table.

CROUPIER. Any other gentlemen care to join? Very well, gentlemen, a new pack, the second game —

VANDALEUR. Wait, I can't see the cards, my eyes are all clouded, red red on the green table — what the hell is the matter — Colquhoun — !

CROUPIER. Might suggest, sir, a pause for refreshment before you continue. . . ?

VANDALEUR. No no no no no no no no —

CROUPIER. Ah — there is the matter of the gentleman's paper — after that side-bet. It won't carry any more.

BAKER-FORTESCUE. I too bear in mind how he crammed his damned Ralahine with Jacobin murderers — threw open the whole of Ireland to republican French anarchy.

VANDALEUR. I — I — my paper — did you say 'no' . . . ?

CROUPIER. We had rather you came back, sir, some other occasion, give us a chance to clear your arrangements with the guarantors you have named. . . ?

VANDALEUR (*very stiff and dignified, standing back from the table*). My estate, my co-operative, everything. . . gone. . . ?

He starts to put on his coat again, and can't manage it, fumbling with coat, hat, shawl, bag, umbrella, dropping them, trembling. He speaks to the audience, while the others freeze.

Emily. Emily Molony. Of the ferocious Molonys, of the ancient clans of Munster, and they changed their religion. Turned her back on me in bed — when I put my hand between her legs, I would have thought she would have bitten it off. . . I am the proprietor, but Craig said, no — president, Craig said — but the people said, no — the committee, the committee went so far as to close the gate. . . Recognize such is now the position. Or else. . . My wife's cousin, not her cousin, she was *murder*, to the committee, they were saved, the estate saved, the state saved by Cicero, so sage a grave statesman. Let the Consuls see to it that the Republic takes no harm — get her out of it, deport her — nigger blood, you can always tell, look at the blue under her finger-nails, the retrograde heels

of her feet who else put the sharp teeth between the legs of
my wife. . . ?

*He drops his coat, bag, hat etc., kicks them away from him,
and stumbles around amongst them.*

> I am the proprietor. I am not. I am nothing.
> I have dropped it on the ground
> I have kicked it around:
> I have given it to all of *you*
> To you all and Fortescue. . .

*He kicks and throws his belongings fiercely from him, making
chaos on the stage. The Faro table is knocked over. He quietens
down.*

It was not to rule Ireland my Anglo-Saxon forebears came in
their black keels to the seacoast of England. . . We should have
kept our own maggots within the putrefying flesh of our own
privy members — not to scatter them broadcast upon the green
fields of the world like God's manna to the men of Israel,
bringing death to the red deer, the trout in the swift rivers, the
seed of the corn before even it springs — creeping heaps of
white poison for those who gather it in baskets. I make desolate.
I abandon.

> Where I go I shall have gone
> And none shall see me ever again. . .

He staggers out. A pause. As he goes, BAKER-FORTESCUE
and the GENTLEMEN *commence a jeering roar which rises
to a ferocious animal climax — then breaks off as* WILBERFORCE
enters, bringing BAKER-FORTESCUE *downstage for an urgent
conversation.*

WILBERFORCE. Tracked the whole thing all the way, Major,
to the declivities of the Hill o' Howth. That goldarn renegade
traitor of a sea-captain sold himself body and soul to your
sweet little mulatto from Boston —

BAKER-FORTESCUE. He has given her the papers — ?

WILBERFORCE. Ah no, at the last minute, refused point-blank
to turn King's Evidence on shore just in case he was double-
crossed — he hands over the papers to no-one save a regular

peace-officer on the quarter-deck of his ship. They made a rendezvous for midnight — ride like hell to the Hill o' Howth — !

BAKER-FORTESCUE. I have no weapons — a gun — a gun — Colquhoun, have you got a gun!

CROUPIER. Nothing here but the old blunderbuss that we use to deter drunks — take it, Major, and welcome — the Major's horse to the door there!

He gives the gun to BAKER-FORTESCUE *from under the table. They go out in a great commotion.*

Scene Nine

The Hill of Howth overlooking Dublin Bay. Moonlight. Enter BAKER-FORTESCUE *with the blunderbuss and* WILBERFORCE *with a pistol.*

BAKER-FORTESCUE. Jamaica — ? You said riots in Jamaica? You said burning — the whole sugar-cane crop destroyed — ? But how — how — ?

WILBERFORCE. We lay for 'em *here* as they come down the lane, ain't no way those guys in the boat behind the breakwater are gonna sus-pect our ambush till it's sprung, and by then it'll be too late, so crouch, Major, crouch. . .

They take up their positions, concealed.

BAKER-FORTESCUE. Goddammit, you must tell me your news from Jamaica!

WILBERFORCE (*whispering*). Ssh, do I hear footsteps. . . ? Not yet. . . Seems like emancipation of all slaves in your British colonies has been rumoured so strongly that the blacks in Jamaica have rose. Your partner in Montego Bay is bankrupt and fled to Mexico.

BAKER-FORTESCUE. What the hell are we doing here then? The money from my sugar-cane was financing my slave-ventures to Cuba — if it's gone who gives a damn for this ship-captain and his King's Evidence?

WILBERFORCE. Way you told it to me it was the profits of
the slave-trade in Cuba was financing your run-down Jamaican
plantations — either way your whole fortune was dependent on
a parcel o' niggers — and by God, Major, the niggers these
days is dead dogs. All you've to look for now is to keep
yourself out of prison, and *that*, Major, is the damn we gotta
give for the King's Evidence. Are you ready, here they come. . .!

ROXANA *and* MICHEAL *enter, with a dark lantern.*

MICHEAL. If there's a Dublin Castle officer on that ship, I'm
not going on till he gets off, I remain in the boat, so, till all's
clear. Do your business with the papers, call me aboard.
You're quite certain this captain has agreed on our passage to
America?

ROXANA. He's a double-dealing rogue, but he knows if he plays
us dirty I can put his neck in a noose and I will. Don't you
worry, we are safe — Where the devil is that boat. . . ?

BAKER-FORTESCUE. Here.

He has come out with his gun behind them. WILBERFORCE
comes out in front, and they see they are trapped.

MICHEAL *opens his mouth to call out, but* WILBERFORCE
*chokes off his yell with his hand over his mouth, then stuffs
a gag in.*

BAKER-FORTESCUE (*to* ROXANA): Now don't *you* call,
Jedediah, because your bully here will hang if you do, and
you know it. Ephraim, your judicial function — secure the
enemies of the public peace.

WILBERFORCE *ties* MICHEAL's *hands, kicks him down and
stoops to tie his ankles.* MICHEAL *kicks.* WILBERFORCE
raises the butt of his pistol to hit him on the head.

No! If you hit him too hard he'll feel sleepy, he'll close his
eyes, we can't have that.

WILBERFORCE *ties* MICHEAL's *feet and feels his clothes.*

WILBERFORCE. He ain't got no papers — so they must be —

BAKER-FORTESCUE. So she has it, so she would have it, *she*

is the mainspring. Emancipation, liberalization, elimination of
all authority — by her own blood she makes mongrels of the
crown of the human race, like an eel climbing a tree, black
and slimy, sticks to the fingers. Ugh. So where is it?

ROXANA. On board ship with the King's Officer, it has already
been delivered, you are too late.

BAKER-FORTESCUE. Oho no, *boy*, I know better. . . Whatever
persuaded you, Jedediah, my little love-pocket, to dress up as
a stinking bitch?

He strokes ROXANA's *neck. She spits at him.*

So, tonight the Rapist Fortescue is going to show you what
is meant by the name he has been given, male or female it's
all one to him, there will be no end to it before death's end —
and your long-tooled Popery bullcalf can glare his eyes out
while I go into you, and then the bullet for *him* too.

*He takes her bonnet off and perches it on his own hat,
crowing like a cock. He then pulls off her shawl and drapes
it around his shoulders. The document falls to the ground.*

WILBERFORCE. Wait a minute, Major, that's it! So we got it —
so we finish — so we don't do no more to 'em — okay —
this is no place for fun and games!

BAKER-FORTESCUE (*draping himself in more of* ROXANA's
clothes). You don't think I came here just to *save* myself,
Wilberforce?

He rams his blunderbuss into ROXANA's *stomach, she falls
on all fours, retching.*

But to *re-affirm* - to lay claim to the whole life they would
have taken away from me — !

*He makes to mount her from behind, crowing like a cock
again. While this has been going on,* ROISIN *has slipped in at
the back, has freed* MICHEAL, *and has sneaked up behind*
BAKER-FORTESCUE *to pick up the blunderbuss.* MICHEAL,
creeping forward, has taken WILBERFORCE's *pistol.*

MICHEAL (*aiming the pistol*). Back, or you're both dead!

WILBERFORCE *and* BAKER-FORTESCUE *spring around to face him.* ROISIN *jams the blunderbuss into* BAKER-FORTESCUE'*s back.*

Roisin, behind me, I'll cover you till you get to the boat —

ROXANA (*scrambles to her feet, grabs the document*). Come, Micheal, the boat — !

She runs out.

ROISIN. You to the boat, you damfool, I've no need for it, *my* place is Ralahine. Keep the pistol, I've got this. Go, go, boy — go! Roxana has the paper — *go*!

MICHEAL *runs after* ROXANA.

BAKER-FORTESCUE. No more than a snot-sucking hunchback — *here* — !

He flings himself at her, and aside as the blunderbuss fires. WILBERFORCE *falls dead. Cries and running feet from offstage* — 'Hold them, halt, in the name of the law' *etcetera.* BAKER-FORTESCUE *grabs* ROISIN. *Enters* 1ST *and* 2ND GENTLEMEN *in great haste.*

1ST GENTLEMAN. Oliver — where are you — good God, what has — ?

BAKER-FORTESCUE. Is he dead, yes he's dead, he was shot by this woman, known associate, I know her, agrarian terrorism — in the name of the King, for a capital crime, I give her in charge.

ROISIN. Roxana, Roxana, I am free — go to the ship — you are safe.

2ND GENTLEMAN *takes her out.*

1ST GENTLEMAN. Are you hurt?

BAKER-FORTESCUE. No.

1ST GENTLEMAN. Perhaps you should have been. Your whole affair, the Duke of Cumberland, the Orange Order, military *coup d'état* — finished. Exposed, Oliver, betrayed, went off before it was ready — they have the documents, everything.

BAKER-FORTESCUE. Everything, all of it, no. . . you said,

'*your* affair'. Your own part in it — not yet public knowledge?

1ST GENTLEMAN (*taking off his Orange sash*). Never will be. Have found it expedient to make my peace with the liberals — has been put to me, very persuasive, for the honour of the Service, preservation of good government, preservation of a gentleman's good name, need be none o' that nonsense about court-martial, any o' that. . . the Duke, most convenient, has inherited the Kingdom of Hanover. He goes over there, for ever. You, being less important — though more important than *me* — Oliver, alas *you* have inherited this. (*He hands* BAKER-FORTESCUE *a pistol*). Understand your financial difficulties in the West Indies have come to a head. Unable to face your creditors. Do the needful. . .

BAKER-FORTESCUE. No.

1ST GENTLEMAN. If you don't, public disgrace. Upon complaints of certain women. From your estates in County Clare. Would you really permit yourself to be drummed out of the regiment for the ravishing of milkmaids?

BAKER-FORTESCUE. No. I mean yes. I mean — oh Lord Christ we went share and share about, even in that, oh Lord Christ, why me and not you — why is it me, me, *me* — ! I won't do it — !

1ST GENTLEMAN. Violation, for the time being, is replaced by seduction. More appropriate for an age of reform. And in the end, even so, the consummation of the longed-for cunt will still be for *us*. Not for you, you're too old, too late, you can't cope, I'm very sorry. . . I made sure it was properly loaded.

BAKER-FORTESCUE. Me, why me, me, ought to be you, you, you —

1ST GENTLEMAN. Not gentlemanly, Oliver, to whimper over your gruel. The Duke said, before he left, that he hoped his friends would understand, but in fact he found most of them were worth no more than a bucket of shit.

He puts his arm round BAKER-FORTESCUE, *kisses him, and goes out.* BAKER-FORTESCUE, *left with the pistol, holds it for a moment in a shaking hand, and moves it shudderingly towards his jaw. The muzzle of the weapon lodges under the jawbone, and before he is ready for it, the trigger jerks and he dies.*

After a pause, BAKER-FORTESCUE *and* WILBERFORCE *rise abruptly from the stage and go off, to clear the scene for the Epilogue.*

Epilogue

The Irish Coast. Enter ROISIN, *as though hanged, her face whitened, and a noose around her neck.*

ROISIN (*sings — air: 'Long Lankin'*):
    'It's an old song and a true song as cold as a bone
    That I cannot stop singing though I am dead and gone.

    I swung from the gallows all tattered and torn:
    The high hope of Ralahine was left all forlorn.'

    Enter CRAIG.

CRAIG. John Scott Vandaleur had disappeared for ever. His wife's relatives, the Molonys, took over the bankrupt estate.

    EMILY *enters, on the opposite side.*

The Anglo-Irish legal system did not recognize the co-operative. Our members were held to be common labourers and that's all, with no rights nor any claim for the improvements they had made to the property. It was legally correct — it was an act of outright robbery — social co-operation at an end, we were remorselessly evicted.

    PEASANTS, *with their bundles, enter slowly, and walk past him. He puts money into their hands.*

I was able, from my own resources, to redeem all the labour-tokens we had issued to the members, in lieu of coin-of-the-realm, for their work on the commune.

EMILY (*deadpan, to the audience*):
    The estate was made safe for my children and their future.
    This could not have been done if my husband, John Vandaleur,
    Had not been regarded, by the Law, as sole proprietor.
    For the loss to these others, I have nothing but grief.
    What else could be done? The estate has been made safe.

She goes out ignoring, and ignored by, the others.

CRAIG (*to the* PEASANTS): My dear friends, before I leave you — I would be most grateful if you would find it possible to subscribe your names for the last time to a formal declaration — I will issue it to the public press.

He hands a paper to the 1ST PEASANT.

1ST PEASANT (*reads*): 'We, the undersigned members of the Ralahine Agricultural and Manufacturing Association, have experienced for the last two years, contentment, peace and happiness under the arrangements introduced by Mr Vandaleur and Mr E. T. Craig.'

One by one they sign the paper, and CRAIG *shakes hands with them.*

CRAIG. Thank you. . . thank you. . . my good friend. . . God bless you. . . God bless you all.

(*To the audience*): Ralahine had been an Irish point of interrogation erected amidst the wilderness of capitalist thought and feudal practice, challenging both in vain for an answer.

The PEASANTS *begin to file out, uttering a muted keen.*

PEASANTS. Sean Vandaleur, why did you go from us. . . ? Why have you left your own Ralahine, Sean Vandaleur. . . ?

CRAIG *goes.*

ROISIN (*sings — air: 'The Red-Haired Man's Wife'*):
They hanged me up high and I swung on the tree:
My brother and his true-love went safe across the sea.

Enter MICHEAL.

MICHEAL (*sings — air: 'The Red-Haired Man's Wife'*):
'O nearer and nearer to the land of America we sailed
The silver and gold of freedom's stronghold did not fail —
If that's what you call such hard work and few dollars to earn
And such news from the shores of Ireland as caused my whole heart-root to burn. . . '

The great hunger, coercion, emigration, rebellion, and the penalties for rebellion — not only my sister — the dark gibbets all over the land. It was brought to me, in America, running out at the scuppers of every ship that dropped anchor. What good, at that time, at that place, to cry to the wind: 'Had Ralahine but been heeded, no famine, no dispersal, no need ever again for Lady Clare and her Brave Boys. . . !' As it was, from all four provinces, in exile we re-gathered, we were re-dedicated, the Fenian Brotherhood, made safe for the cause with great oaths — and we have never to this day given up in the work we put hand to. Let the red soldiers of the red-stained Crown pay heed to us yet.

ROISIN (*sings*):
    'It's an old song and a true song as hot as a fire
    That half-way is no way to attain your desire.

    You know what is needed, you will give it or deny:
    What good for a blind man to open one eye?

    Till we come to our own in our own Irish land
    An old song a true song, will it never have an end. . . ?'

MICHEAL. Our Brotherhood in due course became known as the Republican Brotherhood.

    They go.